Trust, Power and Public Sector Leadership

Trust, Power and Public Sector Leadership: A Relational Approach provides a critical theoretical treatment of trust in the realm of public management and governance.

The public trust agenda is an antidote to rampant bureaucratic control and, in particular, the marketization and instrumentalization associated with New Public Management. The book approaches trust from a relational perspective that draws on insights from trust research, modern sociology and organization and management theory, while lending support to developments in New Public Governance. It provides a theoretical framework that distinguishes between institutional, economic, moral and relational trust and shows how a relational perspective is able to incorporate insights from the other paradigms in an inclusive approach to trust processes. Apart from providing a theoretical reading of the workings of trust in public organizations, the book addresses how trust relates to power and control along with notions of debureaucratization, post-bureaucratic organization and post-heroic leadership. It also shows how the trust agenda, in theory and practice, is related to social capital and thus efforts to strengthen social relations and collaboration in and around public organizations. Speaking of practice, the book takes its empirical point of departure in the Danish public sector. However, the aim of the book is not to promote the "High trust" Danish case as a benchmark or best practice. The aim is to theorize and help make sense of this particular experience by applying general theory to it and extracting general insights – with broader application – from its particular manifestations and outcomes.

There is a need for more elaborate theorizing about trust and power in a public sector setting, and the Danish experience is useful as a starting point for this ambition.

Steen Vallentin is Associate Professor in the Department of Management, Society and Communication at Copenhagen Business School, Denmark. He is Academic Director of the CBS Sustainability center. Apart from trust, his research and teaching is centered on CSR (corporate social responsibility) and developments in the realm of sustainability, with a particular focus on the governmental, political and ideological underpinnings of modern debates about corporate sustainability. His research is published in journals such as *Journal of Trust Research, Organization, Business Ethics Quarterly, Business & Society* and *Journal of Business Ethics*. He has coauthored several Danish-language books and articles about public sector trust.

Routledge Studies in Trust Research

Series editors: Joanna Paliszkiewicz and Kuanchin Chen

Available Titles in this Series:

Trust, Power and Public Sector Leadership
A Relational Approach

Steen Vallentin

NEW YORK AND LONDON

First published 2023
by Routledge
605 Third Avenue, New York, NY 10158

and by Routledge
4 Park Square, Milton Park, Abingdon, Oxon, OX14 4RN

Routledge is an imprint of the Taylor & Francis Group, an informa business

© 2023 Taylor & Francis

Library of Congress Cataloging-in-Publication Data
Names: Vallentin, Steen, author.
Title: Trust, power and public sector leadership : a relational approach / Steen Vallentin.
Description: New York, NY : Routledge, 2023. |
Includes bibliographical references and index.
Identifiers: LCCN 2022020435 | ISBN 9781138364820 (hardback) |
ISBN 9781032363677 (paperback) | ISBN 9780429431104 (ebook)
Subjects: LCSH: Leadership. | Government accountability. | Public trustees.
Classification: LCC HD57.7 .V356 2023 | DDC 303.3/4–dc23/eng/20220518
LC record available at https://lccn.loc.gov/2022020435

ISBN: 978-1-138-36482-0 (hbk)
ISBN: 978-1-032-36367-7 (pbk)
ISBN: 978-0-429-43110-4 (ebk)

DOI: 10.4324/9780429431104

Typeset in Bembo
by Newgen Publishing UK

Contents

Preface

This book builds on a couple of decades worth of engagement with trust as an organizational phenomenon and managerial concern. What for me started out as a broad and for the most part theoretical and conceptual interest rooted in sociological systems theory (Luhmann) later turned into a more focused and applied approach spurred by developments in the Danish public sector under the banner of "Trust reform". Together with colleagues in the Department of Management, Politics and Philosophy at Copenhagen Business School, I have both contributed to and found inspiration in the emergence and development of the public trust agenda. We have (alongside other academics, experts and consultants) contributed with books and other publications on trust and social capital alongside public presentations and teaching. Inspiration has come not only from central and local policy making and trust initiatives, but also, for me personally, from interactions and discussions with students in the Master of Public Governance program over many years. Overall, the trust discourse has had its collective eyes set on enabling more freedom, self-determination and collaboration within and among public organizations – as a pushback against bureaucratic control and New Public Management.

Denmark is internationally known as the "High trust" country par excellence, and the public trust reform is arguably the most ambitious of its kind in the world. However, the Danish experience of public sector trust is, with the odd exception, not well documented in the international research literature and the applied mindset can be part of the explanation for this. The discourse has largely remained domestic with an instrumental focus on results and a strong government (central, local) and labor union imprint. Besides, there is also the question of comparability that often haunts public administration literature. To what extent are the Danish experiences and experiments with trust even transferable or useful in other contexts where different institutional, social and economic conditions prevail?

This book's answer to this question is centered on *theory* and the possibilities of distance and generalization it provides. The aim of the book is not to provide a prescriptive account of the Danish experience or to promote it as a benchmark or best practice, and it does not overwhelm the reader with empirical cases. The aim is rather to theorize and help make sense of this particular experience by applying general theory to it and extracting general insights – with broader application – from its particular manifestations and outcomes. Indeed, there is a need for more elaborate theorizing about trust and power in a public sector setting, and the Danish experience is useful as a starting point for this ambition.

The present author's process of gaining, building and solidifying a theoretical understanding of the lay of the land has arguably been quite slow. This is not to say that a long gestation period is necessarily a bad thing. Slow development has its own advantages. My own understanding has developed in parallel with the empirical field, but sometimes you need a jolt from the outside to help take your understanding to the next level. One such jolt – or critical event – for me was participation in the *Nordic Research Network on Trust Within and Between Organisations* (2011–2014), which was an opportunity not only to have discussions with Nordic trust researchers, but also to meet and engage with some of the leading lights from the FINT (First International Network on Trust) research community. This experience was enormously inspiring and helpful in gaining a deeper understanding of the trust literature and its usefulness in the context of public management and governance.

Teaching is another important source of inspiration for this book. My own understanding has benefited tremendously from teaching "Trust-Based Management" to professionals for more than ten years, and there is certainly an element of *teaching-based research* to many of the bigger and smaller points in this book and how they intersect and connect. Furthermore, feedback from teaching and everything that goes with it has also helped to broaden the scope of theoretical and conceptual engagement and forge relations to developments in management and organization theory more generally.

This is the essence of what the book sets out to do (based on empirical experiences of trust): (1) to dig into the trust literature and showcase its relevance and usefulness for the theory and practice of modern public management and (2) to show how matters of trust and social capital are related to and have affinities with other theoretical and conceptual developments in the field of management and organization, including post-bureaucratic organizational developments and post-heroic leadership. The overall aim is to provide an elaborate and nuanced theoretical account of what trust is or can be inside public organizations, to harness, synthesize and critically reflect on insights from multiple theoretical perspectives and to help connect the many dots.

Steen Vallentin
Copenhagen, June 2022

Acknowledgments

I would like to thank the following people, who directly or indirectly have contributed to the learning process behind this book. Niels Thyge Thygesen for getting the ball rolling on trust, social capital and gift economy many years ago. Christian Tangkjær for many years of co-teaching and countless rewarding conversations. Søren Jagd (d. 2020) and Lars Fuglsang for their coordination of the *Nordic Research Network on Trust Within and Between Organisations* (2011–2014). The many students from the Master of Public Governance at Copenhagen Business School who have taken – and contributed to – the elective on "Trust-Based Management" over the years. The following people have contributed with concrete empirical inputs and theoretical ideas and inspirations large and small: Carsten Haurum, Elsebeth Henriksen, Anders Mærkedahl Pedersen, Bettina Ruben, Karen Sonne, Ulla Johansen, Søren Obed Madsen, Pernille Steen Pedersen, Mollie Painter and Lot Elshuis.

1 Approaching Public Sector Trust

"Trust", Niklas Luhmann writes, "is a basic fact of social life". In the throes of a complete absence of trust, human beings would hardly be able to get out of bed in the morning, they would "be prey to a vague sense of dread, to paralysing fears" (2017, p. 5). Without *any* trust, Luhmann reminds us, people would not even be able to locate a basis for distrusting others (a pertinent point in these polarizing times). There would be nothing to hold onto, no way to anchor feelings of distrust toward other people, the state, government, authorities, institutions, society, "the system". You need to have trust in something. Otherwise, you are exposed to unmitigated complexity, paralysis and fear. This is not just a matter of human psychology and individual being-in-the-world. Trust is in many ways fundamental to human coexistence. Indeed, trust is "essential for stable relationships, vital for the maintenance of cooperation, fundamental for any exchange and necessary for even the most routine of everyday interactions" (Misztal, 1996, p. 12). Elements of trust are woven into the norms, values, institutions and technologies of modern societies. At the most general societal level, trust is associated with benevolence and goodwill among people, with community and social cohesion, with human well-being and sense of security, well-functioning institutions and social order. "High trust" is what characterizes some (but not all) of the best functioning nation-states and economies in the world (Fukuyama, 1995).

However, apart from generalized trust, we can speak of trust in more particular ways. Trust inside organizations being one such particular. We may then ask: to what extent is trust a basic fact of social life in organizations? Many would be inclined to give an affirmative answer. It is difficult to imagine organizational life bereft of trust, and trust is routinely touted as an important managerial and organizational value. However, taking a closer look, the answer to the question is by no means straightforward. Not only because there is no shared agreement on what trust is or ought to be, but also because developments in modern management theories and practices tend to leave less rather than more room for trust to make a positive difference. Following Ghoshal (2005), trust is one of the first casualties of the diffusion of models of management and governance based on neoclassical economic theory and perpetuating negative economic assumptions about human behavior. According to the tenets of principal-agent theory and transaction cost economics,

DOI: 10.4324/9780429431104-1

human actors/economic agents are self-interested opportunists, acting upon asymmetrical information under conditions of moral hazard. The message is that managers cannot be trusted to do their jobs, and that managers should not put too much trust in their employees either. What is needed instead is authority and monitoring, command and control (Ghoshal, 2005).

This is a book about trust in and around public organizations, and New Public Management (NPM) is, alongside the use of economic modelling in planning and policy-making, the most significant manifestation of the economizing tendency in the public sector (cf. Pedersen, 2011). Bouckaert (2012b, p. 98) speaks of how, "In theory, and in some [public administration] practices" we have seen a movement "from a traditional bureaucracy to a managerial system and from a managerial system to an economic system", the latter movement signifying a shift from "managerial thinking to an economic paradigm based on public choice, principal-agent relations and transaction cost economics". This indicates the severity, if you will, of the economic challenge to trust in the public sector. However, operative words in Bouckaert's formulation are "*in theory* and in *some practices*". In our view, the public sector and its organizations are not reducible to economic systems. We consider public organizations as managerial and social systems that incorporate bureaucratic and economic elements, and we consider trust as a problematic that needs to be considered in the context of managerial and organizational intersections of hierarchy and market (cf. Adler, 2001).

In other words, we need to account for the workings of NPM as a challenge to trust, but in doing so we need not succumb to a grand narrative of neoliberal takeover of the public sector (cf. Siltala, 2013). Although NPM is a powerful force, it is not everything that the public sector is – neither in theory nor in practice. In some countries, there is pushback against negative effects of NPM (see below), and the models and tools of NPM are continually challenged by other models and philosophies of management and leadership that are more conducive to trust and recognize its importance for organizational relations and performance. Indeed, there is a tug-of-war going on between different public governance models and ideas about reform, and this creates a complex and layered reality in modern public organizations (Hartley, 2005). As Christensen and Lægreid (2011) have pointed out, there is both an NPM reform wave and a post-NPM reform wave to account for (although the contours and accomplishments of the latter are arguably rather blurry compared to the former). While the NPM reform wave is a reaction to managerial challenges and governance problems of the "old public administration", the post-NPM reform wave is partly a reaction to the negative effects of NPM. Together, they result "in a complex sedimentation or layering of structural and cultural features" (Christensen & Lægreid, 2011, p. 408). NPM is thus challenged by other public management discourses (Plotnikof, 2016). There are alternatives.

What we need to understand better, then, is how trust is conditioned and constrained in modern public organizations, for example, how it is incentivized (or disincentivized) and associated with risk and opportunity. Solomon and

Flores (2001) give the organizational workings of trust a Hobbesian – and somewhat melodramatic – spin to underscore its significance:

> Without trust, the corporate community is reduced to a group of resentful wage slaves and defensive, if not ambitious, managers. People will do their jobs, but they will not offer their ideas, or their enthusiasm, or their souls. Without trust the corporation becomes not a community but a brutish state of nature, a war of all against all in which employment tends to be nasty, brutish, and short.
>
> (p. 5)

Going back to the initial remarks from Luhmann regarding the human paralysis that would result from a complete absence of trust, it is an interesting thought experiment to imagine organizations *sans* trust. Although Solomon and Flores (2001) have private businesses in mind in the above quotation, the fallout would most likely be the same in public organizations: much would be lost due to lack of collaboration, mutual identification, motivation and engagement. We might even hypothesize that absent any trust, most organizations would simply stop functioning and collapse. This can serve as a poignant reminder of the importance of trust for human well-being as well as organizational performance.

However, the problem with such a black and white, either/or view of trust is that it is too reductive and out of touch with the social complexities surrounding trust. Trust is not an unequivocal social or moral good in organizations. It can be blind and thoughtless, pathological even (Baier, 1986; Gargiulo & Ertug, 2006). It can be functional or dysfunctional (Oomsels et al., 2019). Trust has multiple meanings, antecedents and forms of attribution, and it is surrounded by functional equivalents and placeholders, that is, alternative ways to absorb complexity and support action. We need to understand it in relation to its most obvious opposite, distrust, and in the forms of low trust and lack of trust (that need not imply distrust). And we need to relate it to matters of power and control. It is one thing to acknowledge that trust will almost always be present in some form in modern organizations, another to suggest that there is enough of it or to have the willingness and ability to work toward creating more trust. What does it even mean to manage trust, considering that trust cannot be imposed on others, forced or bought? To iterate, the answer to the question of whether or how trust is a basic fact of social life in organizations is a complicated one, shrouded in ambiguities and paradoxes.

In this book, our focus is on the ambiguities and paradoxes that accrue to trust in public organizations. Our aim is to contribute to a better and more elaborate understanding of trust and its theoretical and practical entanglements in a public sector setting. For this purpose, we build on extant scholarship on trust, power and public administration along with literature on social capital and management and leadership studies. Hence, we make a virtue out of combining insights from different academic disciplines. Although trust is an often touted feature of public sector management, there is arguably a lack of sustained scholarly reflection on the workings of trust (we outline some of the reasons below). Building on and expanding extant scholarship, our aim is to add more theoretical substance and critical and constructive reflection to this discussion.

Before we continue on this path, however, we need to take a step back and consider the different ways in which matters of trust are addressed in regard to the public sector. This will help clarify and position the approach taken in this book.

The Public Sector, Trust and COVID-19

Following Bouckaert (2012b), we can speak of three types of relationships with regard to the public sector and trust: (1) T1 – trust of citizens and organizations toward government and the public sector, (2) T2 – trust of government and the public sector toward citizens and organizations and (3) T3 – trust within government and the public sector. While public administration research has predominantly been concerned with the first type of relationship (ibid.), our focus in this book is the third type: the *internal* workings of trust and how trust is woven into efforts to make organizational change happen in the public sector. T3 encompasses both intra- and interorganizational relationships within and among public sector organizations. Our primary focus will be intraorganizational processes, but our theoretical treatment will touch on both types of relationships.

Our focus on T3 does not mean that we disregard the highly material concerns of T1 and T2. As mentioned, public administration research has primarily been concerned with T1 relationships (Bouckaert, 2012b). In the words of Pearce (2008, p. 481): "Governments, at least the non-kleptocracies, exist to produce trust: trust in fellow citizens, trust in contracts and the rule of law, and trust that governments will meet their responsibilities to serve and protect." A key starting point for the 2010 Organisation for Economic Co-operation and Development (OECD) Ministerial Conference was that "trust, built on openness, integrity, and transparency, remains an overarching goal to foster an effective and performance-driven public sector, delivering better public services more efficiently, and promoting open and transparent government" (OECD, 2011, p. 7). A more recent report from the Joint Research Centre under the European Commission suggests that:

> Trust contributes to forming positive, reciprocal ties with other people and increases the willingness of people to act in favour of the community. It is not only believed to be the main contributor in the process of building of social capital but in economic exchanges, by increasing predictability, stability, civic engagement and collective collaboration, it reduces transactions costs, facilitates cooperation with other people (information flow), creates confidence in the regulatory capacity of

public institutions and contributes to the general feeling of community and belonging.

(Weziak-Bialowolska & Dijkstra, 2015, p. 1)

T1 reflects important agendas regarding anti-corruption, transparency, accountability and the basic functioning of the public sector and its relations to civil society (European Commission, 2017; OECD, 2017). However, trust can sometimes seem like a scarce commodity, as if there is never enough of it. T1 is thus reflective of the "trust crisis" as one of the multiple crises that modern societies are engulfed in and have to cope with. It signifies widespread distrust of the populace toward governments, politicians and other authorities. We live in an era of widespread polarization, tribalism and "us vs. them" identity politics – fueled by the echo chambers of social media. This often leaves little room for meaningful democratic conversation and bipartisan collaboration, let alone for trust to flourish. As Luhmann (2017, p. 57) points out, "Trust is only possible where truth is possible, where people can reach agreement about any given entity which is binding upon a third party."

The COVID-19 crisis has served as a gargantuan stress test and social experiment putting renewed emphasis on T1 and T2 relationships all over the world. The pandemic and responses to the pandemic constitute a historically unprecedented explicitization and test of trust relations between governments, health authorities and citizens. It has showcased (and continues to showcase) both the benefits of trust and the damage done by distrust – along with the manifold social ambiguities of trust. It has forced politicians and government officials to assess, often on a day-to-day basis, how trustworthy citizens are and to what extent not only guidelines but also rules and controls are necessary to assure their responsible behavior – or curb their irresponsible behavior. And it has made it apparent for citizens how political decisions are made regarding pandemic responses and public health, with urgency, uncertainty and incomplete knowledge as constant challenges to consistency, meaningfulness and trustworthiness.

Although this is not a book about the COVID-19 crisis, we need to take account of how the pandemic experience will most likely have lasting effects on the organization of work and the structural conditions for trust in and around organizations. Apart from illuminating issues of trust (and distrust) in relations between government, public authorities and citizens, the crisis has forced organizations across the board to experiment with new forms of organization of work, that is, people working from home, virtual workforces and hybrid management at a distance. The pandemic has imposed trust on organizations in the sense that many job functions have been freed from ordinary forms of managerial oversight. Indeed, managers have to some extent been forced to relinquish control and rely more on the self-managing and -motivating capacities of employees. Outcomes have differed and we do not yet have anything resembling an overview of the amassed experiences. However, there is little doubt that there will be long-lasting effects from this and that different scenarios are imaginable: both ones that leave more room for trust and ones that leave less.

Trust and Public Administration

Our focus on T3 relationships indicates that this is a book about trust in organizations rather than trust at a societal level. To iterate, it is a book about the functions and managerial aspects of trust in modern public organizations. Although it is mainly a theoretical book offering a conceptual treatment, our approach is rooted in and inspired by practical developments in Northern Europe in particular. In some countries with strong welfare legacies, like Denmark, Sweden and Norway, trust has, in recent years, become a label for a new brand of reform aiming to debureaucratize and decentralize the public sector while, ideally, paving the way for more trusting relationships to develop between managers and employees and between different public functions and organizations. One espoused aim has been to give public sector employees more freedom to act – to make them more self-managing and better able to exercise their professional judgment in their daily work and encounters with citizens. This in turn should enable better utilization of their resources and more efficient creation of public value. Furthermore, the focus on trust has been an integral part of efforts to reach out to civil society and engage volunteers – and thus networks – in collaborative production and delivery of services. Importantly, the internal perspective on trust and trust reform is not, so to speak, about trust for the sake of trust in some altruistic sense. A common thread in the promotional efforts that we have seen in Scandinavia is the belief that trust – alongside other managerial concepts stressing the value of relationship-building (such as social capital and co-creation) – is conducive to higher performance, to better and more efficient use of taxpayer money, to doing more with less.

Internal trust reform may for the time being be a particular Scandinavian phenomenon that to some extent reflects the high trust conditions prevailing in the Scandinavian countries (Fukuyama, 1995). However, as already indicated, the turn to trust in these settings is motivated by a more general concern: widespread discontent with decades of public sector reform dominated by NPM. Hood and Dixon (2015a) present an analysis of three decades of successive NPM-style reforms in the UK (for many the vanguard state of NPM). They conclude that while NPM was ostensibly meant to create "a government that works better and costs less", it has instead led to higher costs and more complaints. With its firm focus on managing and measuring performance outcomes and its insistence that disaggregation and competition in public services are conducive to lower costs and higher quality, NPM-type measures have had deeply negative effects on many important administrative values. Indeed, with their excessive emphasis on cost cutting, NPM reforms have not only been blind to the value of cooperation across public agencies, thus undermining trust, they have also, according to Hood and Dixon (2015b, p. 265), "damaged some traditional and important 'Weberian' qualities of administration such as fairness and consistency". Damage to trust – and other values associated with the "warm hands" of public welfare (Clarke & Newman, 1997) – is part and parcel of the general critique of NPM for being too reliant upon a managerial and instrumental mindset (Christensen & Lægreid, 2007; Pollitt & Bouckaert, 2011).

In this book, we explicitly consider trust as a possible solution to problems in public sector organizations. Hence, it is one thing to acknowledge that NPM can do damage to trust, collaboration and motivation, another to turn to trust and trust-based leadership for solutions to this problem. It is one thing to consider lack of trust as symptomatic of how the public sector has developed over the last couple of decades, another to see explicit efforts to build trust as the remedy. Indeed, trust is a topic often neglected by public administration/management scholars (Oomsels et al., 2019). One explanation for this is a tendency in political science to define trust as naïve and unconditional while considering skepticism and distrust as positives (Six, 2013). In parallel, economists tend to define trust in rationalistic and opportunistic terms that strongly resemble – and prescribe – a distrustful disposition, with some arguing that trust is best reserved for intimate and personal relationships, outside the hustle and bustle of professional life, markets and modern organizations (see Chapter 2 – for a recent attempt to address and remedy shortcomings of economic theory with regard to trust, see Herold, 2019).

Hence, it is not unreasonable to claim that there is an intellectual bias against trust in parts of the public administration literature and that key assumptions in political science and economics tend to make these disciplines blind to the possible benefits of trust. Although such skepticism can certainly be warranted, based on practical experiences and empirical observation, we take a different starting point. Theoretically, we approach trust from the point of view of a reflexive sociology, aiming to provide a nuanced and balanced account of its pros and cons and how it relates to other concepts and phenomena in the realm of organization, management and leadership. We basically want to understand what trust is and does (or *can* be and *can* do), for better or worse, in public sector organizations. We are aware that reflexive sociology can be many things. According to Wacquant (1992), it is a label that is vague to the point of near vacuity. We associate it with an eclectic approach that combines different sociological perspectives (ranging from Luhmann to Bourdieu) and puts emphasis on the significance of self-reference, self-awareness and self-critique in scholarly work. Furthermore, we associate reflexive sociology with an awareness of how the knowledge generated by social science can be "injected" back into the reality it describes, and can have performative effects (ibid.). This is akin to Giddens' notion of "the double hermeneutic", that is, the realization that the

> theories and findings of the social sciences cannot be kept wholly separate from the universe of meaning and action which they are about. But, for their part, lay actors are social theorists, whose theories help to

constitute the activities and institutions that are the object of study of specialized social observers or social scientists. There is no clear dividing line between informed sociological reflection carried on by lay actors and similar endeavours on the part of specialists.

(Giddens, 1984, pp. xxxii–xxxiii)

In other words, "sociology is a reflection on practices that are themselves self-reflective" (Bauman, 1978, p. 160). Trust is subject to social theorizing by lay actors – organizational members – all the time, and the sociological lens must be able to include such theorizing/theories-in-use in its field of study (cf. Argyris & Schön, 1974). This adds another layer to the problematic regarding the manifold meanings of trust and the challenges involved in creating some sort of shared meaning regarding trust – in spite of people's different understandings, lived experiences and dispositions. While trust certainly lends itself to theoretical idealization, the relevance and usefulness of such idealizations must be considered in relation to the practical experiences of trust in organizations. A reflexive sociological vantage point thus allows us to capture both the ideal and the real aspects of trust as a social phenomenon (see below) – that is, both the ideal normative values and prescriptions it embodies and its real social functioning and entanglements.

Trust and Public Sector Reform

As indicated, our treatment of trust in a public sector setting is inspired by institutional developments in Scandinavia, first and foremost Denmark. This has a number of implications for our treatment of trust – as will be apparent throughout the book. For now, it suffices to say that the case of Denmark provides a high trust starting point for theorizing trust (Fukuyama, 1995), and that the public sector in an affluent and leading modern welfare state such as Denmark is recognized as a site of management and leadership – comparable to the private sector. That being said, it would be misleading to suggest that this book represents an unashamedly Danish approach to trust and public sector management. While building, implicitly and explicitly, on the Danish experience (vis-à-vis the double hermeneutic), our theoretical aim is not to provide a prescriptive account of this experience or to promote it as a benchmark or best practice. Our theoretical aim is rather to theorize and help make sense of this particular experience by applying general theory to it and extracting general insights from its particular manifestations and outcomes. Indeed, we see a need for more elaborate theorizing about trust in a public sector setting, and we use the Danish experience as a starting point for this ambition.

At the face of it, the Danish trust reform is arguably the most ambitious of its kind in the world so far. It has involved multilevel engagement of central and local government along with mobilization of trust-based initiatives in public organizations. Although there have been earlier rumblings of discontentment over the implications of NPM in Denmark, the trust agenda got its first formal thrust forward after the parliamentary election and change of government in 2011. The newly elected government, led by the Social Democrats with support from the Social Liberals and the Socialist People's Party, made trust-based reform of the public sector an explicit priority. The Danish government platform of October 6, 2011 thus speaks of a pressing need to debureaucratize the public sector – in order to counteract many years of growing bureaucracy and state control over municipalities in particular. Controls that do not directly benefit the purpose of providing value for citizens should be abandoned and this should leave more room for trust to develop and be an asset (Den danske regering, 2011). In June 2013, symptomatic of the Danish tradition of cross-sector dialogue and labor market negotiation, the trust agenda became part of a collective agreement between national government, Local Government Denmark (Kommunernes Landsforening – the national advocacy organization of Danish municipalities), Danish Regions (the advocacy organization for the regions, which are responsible for the provision of hospital services) and three labor unions – Akademikerne, FTF and OAO. This agreement (Regeringen et al., 2013), which addresses the need for modernization of the public sector and proposes that "management and governing should have trust and responsibility as their point(s) of departure", has subsequently been referred to as "The trust reform". The Liberal-Conservative governments in office from 2015 to 2019 maintained the focus on trust and the need to simplify rules and procedures in the public sector in order to allow public employees to focus more on their core tasks and less on documentation and paperwork. The current Social Democratic government led by Prime Minister Mette Frederiksen has kept the trust flag high and has come up with new initiatives supporting local self-government among municipalities – freed, to some extent, from the constraints of centralized state bureaucracy and rule-following (see Chapter 5).

To iterate, while the Danish trust trajectory has provided inspiration for the storyline of this book and serves as an empirical reference point throughout our treatment, we do not approach it – or present it – as a best practice, benchmark or example to follow in other countries. Or that is not our primary aim. Although it is useful for showcasing the potential of working with trust, its various outcomes are contested and it has certainly not been an unequivocal success. Thus, it is doubtful whether it has led to more fundamental disruptions of the normal workings of governance and management. While debureaucratization of the public sector remains on the agenda of national government, it is challenged by other policy prerogatives that tend to point in other directions and often turn out to have greater leverage. Trust is but one of several reform agendas to which public organizations and their managers and employees are continuously subjected. Furthermore, both the collective agreement and the policy priorities of recent governments suggest that trust-as-reform is a complement to rather than a substitute for existing models of management and governance. The same institutional pattern is seen in local policy-making.

The Municipality of Copenhagen has led the way among public organizations when it comes to addressing the relevant trust issues in a programmatic fashion. Hence, in its budget agreement for 2013, the political leadership vowed to "remove all unnecessary controls and bureaucracy" and give employees more freedom and time to carry out their core tasks (instead of filling out forms and documenting their activity for control purposes, etc.; Københavns Kommune, 2012, p. 69). According to this document, the Municipality of Copenhagen is setting an explicit trust agenda and striving to create rule-free areas and trustful spaces for its managers to manage and its employees to self-manage (aims that have been reaffirmed in other more recent communications). However, it is also clearly stated that the turn to trust is not about removing all rules and control requirements. The purported aim is to get rid of "unnecessary controls" – however, they may be defined and separated from supposedly "necessary" ones. The budget agreement for 2016 purports that the trust agenda is all about mutual commitment and collaboration involving politicians, managers and employees, and that this in turn requires strong working communities focusing on the core task and characterized by high job satisfaction, good working environments and an inclusive and engaging work culture (Københavns Kommune, 2015). More recently, these ideas have been brought to bear in the adoption of a "Charter on working communities" that explicitly build on and extend the municipality's prior commitments regarding trust (Københavns Kommune, 2019 – see Chapter 5).

Trust, Power and Control

These are illustrative examples of how practice (or certainly policy) and theory are intertwined. They capture a central theme in this book and the crux of our argument. Trust does not constitute some hallowed ground where the workings of power are somehow short-circuited or pushed aside. We need to consider trust and power as two sides of the same coin, as intertwined and interrelated organizational concepts and phenomena. This is worth noting as there is a tendency in the scholarly trust literature to disregard matters of power, and for the literature on power to pay little attention to trust. Research that explicitly connects trust and power is surprisingly rare. This was pointed out by Möllering (2019) in a recent editorial in *Journal of Trust Research*. This is not to say that there is a complete absence of cross-cutting reflection, but it is arguably an area of concern that calls for more explicit articulation and attention. Not least when it comes to understanding the workings of trust in organizations.

One defining characteristic of public sector organizations is that they are politically controlled. Power, politics and public accountability are built into their modus operandi. It is hard to even imagine a public sector running entirely on trust, if that is taken to mean: without some form of managerial oversight, economic budgeting and planning, documentation and control – not to mention legally binding rules and regulations. As indicated, this is not what trust reform entails. It is not about throwing the baby out with the bath water. It is about finding new, smarter, more effective ways to balance trust and power and integrate trust into existing systems and modes of management and governance. Hence, the choice is not between trust *or* power. Instead, we must strive to understand the complex interrelations between trust *and* power. We believe that the strength of this approach is that it aligns well with the practical challenges facing trust in modern organizations. A potential weakness is that it makes the message of trust less straightforward and more complex and blurry. Vis-à-vis our focus on T3 relationships, party politics and the political game itself are not central analytical concerns in this book. However, we do need to take account of political power as a conditioning and constraining factor for governance and management in politically controlled organizations.

While broader reflections on trust and power are scarce, the scholarly literature does provide a solid basis for reflecting on relations between trust and control, the so-called trust-control nexus (see Chapter 3). Möllering (2019) suggests that research has perhaps presumed that in dealing with control it was already including power in its considerations. But, as he also points out (and we agree), it is not as simple as that. There is more to power than control, not least when it comes to capturing managerial aspects of how trust relates to power. So, on the one hand, more elaborate theorizing is needed regarding the trust-power relationship. On the other, the literature on the trust-control nexus is an important entry point for an understanding of trust in public sector organizations. Hence, we concur with Edelenbos and Eshuis (2012, p. 651), who argue that "one-sided attention to either control or trust does not do justice to the complexity of the practice of public management. In practice, public managers have to deal with the complex interplay between trust and control all the time." The trust-control nexus points to one of the main queries in the trust literature: whether trust and control should be considered as substitutes or in more complementary or mutually constitutive terms. Supporting a substitution view, some research has shown that formal control mechanisms, involving the codification, monitoring and safeguarding of social relations, can undermine or chase out trust, while other contributions have pointed to situations in which trust seems to remove the need for control (Bijlsma-Frankema & Costa, 2005; Khodyakov, 2007). In relation to public management, the substitutive view implies that strengthening of trust weakens control and vice versa (Edelenbos & Eshuis, 2012). However, theory development and empirical studies are increasingly supporting the view that trust and control are not substitutes, but complements (Six, 2013).

We propose that a complementary view has greater value and relevance for an understanding of the workings of trust in public sector organizations. To iterate, we argue for the value of considering trust-based reform initiatives not as a matter of replacing control with trust, but as a matter of reconfiguring and balancing intricate relationships between trust and control (Vallentin & Thygesen, 2017). This is supported more broadly by research that recognizes how trust and control both serve to enable the effective functioning of individuals, teams and organizations and how both constitute essential features of organizational life (Costa & Bijlsma-Frankema, 2007).

Two Meanings of "Relational"

In this book, we approach public sector management and governance from a relational perspective. The basic relational creed, if you will, is well expressed in this quote from Gergen (1999 – quoted in Gittell, 2006):

> If we hold the individual to be the fundamental atom of society, so do we emphasize separation as opposed to community (...) As a result we give little attention to relations – to the coordinated efforts required, for example, to generate knowledge, reason and morality (...) We emphasize individual rights while paying little attention to the duties required to sustain our communities (...) Attention to individual units leads to blindness of relationship.
>
> (p. 18)

The same point holds true for organizations: it makes a difference whether you start with the (atomistic) individual or with the relations that hold individuals together and constitute their organizational coexistence. Gittell (2006) speaks of how there is a tendency to overlook the relational basis of human identity in our individualist societies, while also arguing that the way people work together cannot be fully understood without a relational perspective. Although we explicitly recognize that different theoretical perspectives and sets of assumptions can complement each other and serve to improve our understanding, we strongly emphasize the insights provided by a relational understanding. Thus, we concur with Ospina and Uhl-Bien (2012, p. xxi), who argue that "As we have entered the twenty-first century, issues of relationality have become more evident and are now paramount in the attention of those experiencing the reality (and practice) of leadership."

Some of our relational points regarding trust, and many of the points made in this book regarding organization, management and leadership, have more general application. They do not apply exclusively to public sector organizations, but to other forms of organization as well. Thus, we are not suggesting that trust in the public sector context differs fundamentally from trust in other organizational/managerial settings. Here, as elsewhere, we can speak of the prevalence of institution-based, calculus-based and relational trust (Rousseau et al., 1998). However, our sociological lens alerts us to the fact that these basic forms of trust are not just reflective of individual (psychological) predispositions. They are embedded in particular ways in the history and development of public governance. The three forms are institutionalized in the classical or Neo-Weberian model of public administration (institution-based) and in the modes of governing associated with NPM (calculus-based) and New Public Governance ([NPG] relational) (Bouckaert, 2012a, 2012b; Van de Walle, 2011). Hence, it is the interplay of different embedded forms of trust that we need to understand better – with regard to theory as well as practice.

At the level of governance archetypes, we build our argument on the relational view of trust with its roots in sociology and its affinities with developments in NPG – a governance paradigm that is supportive of a relational and networked view of the public sector and its – preferably self-governing – organizations. NPG is rooted in the disciplines of organizational sociology and network theory, while also being indebted to the literature on organizational social capital. It acknowledges the fragmented and uncertain nature of modern public management and taps into recent developments in management theory that are concerned with creating "the relational organization". With its emphasis on the forging of strong and enduring intra- and interorganizational relationships and the governance of processes, it makes room for trust and relational capital to act as core governance mechanisms (Osborne, 2006). That is, at least in principle it does. Not surprisingly perhaps, considering the proposed bias in political science, even the literature on NPG tends to ascribe limited significance to trust per se.

Importantly, we are not just arguing that a relational view of trust is superior compared to alternatives. As indicated in our brief discussions of power and control, we take a position that does not allow us to define NPM as the enemy of trust, plain and simple – or, for that matter, NPG as the necessary solution. While the relational view does embody a set of normative values and prescriptions regarding trust, it also provides us with a vantage point for reflecting on, again, different institutionalized views of trust in public organization, how they intersect and interact and how they can be combined in hybrid forms.

Hence, we make dual use of the notion of "relational" (see also Sheppard & Sherman, 1998, on *relational grammars* of trust and their roots in different forms of human interdependence). On the one hand, it designates a particular view of trust that differs from institutional and economic alternatives. On the other, we use it to signify a vantage point for meta-theoretical reflection on how different views of trust are constituted and how they intersect and interact. In other words, our reflexive sociological interest is not limited to promotion of a relational view. The relational view is an embodiment of the value of social and thus interpersonal trust among individuals – managers and employees. It represents a foregrounding of (social) trust as a tangible and important managerial concern and something to which we can attribute managerial agency. It is made visible through corporate codes espousing the relational value of trust and, most significantly, through the talk and action of managers practicing trust-based leadership in some form. However, in theorizing trust in public organizations, we cannot limit ourselves to its most obvious, visible and personalized manifestations. Unlike the relational view, the institutional and economic alternatives tend to relegate trust to the background in the sense that they rely on (impersonal) system trust – bureaucratic structures, norms, values and contractual safeguards – rather than social trust. This does not make them irrelevant for our consideration of trust-based leadership, though. The point being that even those who are less (or not at all) inclined to talk about trust and its possible merits in regard to public administration can be seen to subscribe to a particular theory or a particular set of assumptions about trust (vis-à-vis our earlier point about theories-in-use). To iterate, what we find on the other side of relational trust is not just conventional, repressive forms of authority, power and control. We find other views of trust that we need to account for and thus include in our theoretical framework.

What the reflexive sociological lens provides us with is a starting point for theorizing different perspectives on trust, their underlying assumptions and their social implications. It is not just about capturing a particular (relational) theory of trust, it is also about providing a meta-theoretical basis for understanding the different theories of trust that are enacted, explicitly or implicitly, in public organizations. Thus, we present a framework distinguishing between *institutional, economic, moral* and *relational* trust (see Chapter 2), and we argue that these forms are at work alongside each other, simultaneously, and that they have paradigmatic properties in the sense that they each provide a particular way of defining and valuing trust and particular recipes for action. As we will show, the tug-of-war between different views of trust constitutes a battle over the hearts and minds of public sector managers and employees involving deep-seated assumptions about human behavior and motivation.

The Ideal, the Real and the Elusiveness of Trust

That being said, our treatment of trust in this book undeniably straddles the is/ought distinction. It represents a dual investment in trust. We contribute and take a stand in regard to highly normative matters while maintaining a critical, analytical and explorative interest in how different notions of trust and power are at play in the theory and practice of public administration. Thus, the relational view does embrace the positive associations of trust, ranging from benevolent notions of "the social", social interaction and social exchange to collaboration, community, mutual commitment and norms of reciprocity. It gives primacy to consensus and unanimity over conflicting interests and diversity of values. This reflects an underlying cultural disposition that ascribes meaning, value and potential for change and development to such, if you will, post-bureaucratic features of modern organization. As indicated, this cultural disposition is strongly indebted to the norms and values of liberal democracy in general and the modern welfare state in particular.

It also implies that we approach trust-based leadership as a social practice through and through – as opposed to one that is centered on the individual. It is characteristic of some of the popular (American) management literature on trust that it builds on and perpetuates strong norms of individuality and self-development. Trust then becomes a matter of starting with self, building a particular mindset and consequently bringing it to bear in managerial action – with organizational others mostly being considered as potential barriers standing in the way of whatever the individual manager wants to accomplish (Covey & Link, 2013). Our starting point is different and has close affinities with notions such as distributed leadership (Spillane, 2005) and shared leadership (Fletcher, 2004; Fletcher & Käufer, 2003). Although we acknowledge the importance of the personal dimension and personal leadership in trust (as in leading by example), we put more emphasis on leadership as an inclusive process and collective – and thus relational – accomplishment. This again reflects a certain cultural disposition in favor of community, inclusiveness and low power distance. However, keeping in mind our critical analytical interest in trust, we will also reflect on the ways in which relational trust in practice often fails to live up to its theoretical promises. Or, more precisely, how trust-based initiatives that build on relational principles in practice can turn out to have unintended or unforeseen consequences that are in conflict with such principles. Furthermore, we will point to some of the built-in contradictions, tensions and paradoxes that come with trust-based leadership. For example, trust-based leadership can be seen both as an embodiment of heroic leadership (leading by example) and post-heroic leadership (taking a step back and motivating others to contribute). The paradox is that it may be considered a heroic act to be willing and able to step back and let others flourish and perhaps take credit for the collective outcome. It can be an act of heroism for managers to dare appear non-heroic to their surroundings (unless it is all too apparently part of a self-affirming heroic narrative). We will treat this problematic as a matter of managerial self-representation (see Chapter 6).

It is par for the course for modern leaders – who want to portray themselves as strong, dynamic, innovative, transformational – to espouse trust as a managerial value or virtue. This is another reason why it is all too easy to take trust for granted. In a dynamic and constantly changing world, strong leaders need to show trust and delegate responsibilities to capable followers in order to inspire, empower and motivate them and make the best possible use of their resources. And followers need to trust their capable leaders. This is the standard recipe found in popular management literature. The problem with this sort of standard version is that it tends to make trust seem too easy and self-evident while glossing over many of the intricate social mechanisms that play a part in making or breaking trust. It perpetuates a reductive either/ or view of trust (as different from distrust – or power/control) and with it we run the risk of supporting a heroic and myopic view of the modern leader as the ultimate source or cause of organizational trust. In the management literature, we see a tendency to, on the one hand, acknowledge the importance of trust (what would the alternative be?), while, on the other, devoting little attention to it. When all else is said and done, trust is also important – often seems to be the underlying message. The result being that trust effectively becomes a sort of residual or peripheral concern. An espoused value-word rather than something that calls for concerted managerial and organizational attention and action.

In its most idealized forms, trust can appear to be a "magic concept", that is, a concept characterized by its broad scope, great flexibility and a positive spin or normative charge that does not easily admit opposites that people would want to support (Pollitt & Hupe, 2011). However, speaking of trust in regard to government and the public sector, at least one magical element is missing. Pollitt and Hupe (2011) suggest that magic concepts share the following characteristics: (1) *broadness*, (2) *normative attractiveness*, (3) *implication of consensus* and (4) *global marketability*. So far, trust certainly fails to be fashionable in a globally marketable way. And the implication of consensus often seems to be more a matter of symbolism and outward appearances than deeply rooted in organizational perceptions and practices.

This point leads directly to another vital challenge for the use of trust in organizations: the multiple meanings of the word/notion/concept. There are two aspects to this problematic. One is conceptual/theoretical, the other is cultural. Both have to do with people's different common sense experiences of interpersonal trust. Trust is in the eyes of the beholder in the sense that it is a form of social attribution (you can choose to have trust in others and act with trust toward others – trust cannot be forced upon you from the outside). It is misleading to suggest that we all have our own subjective theory of trust, but people do have their own common sense, more or less articulated sense of what trust is to them – that reflects their lived experience and may or may not fit into a particular theoretical category. A problem with trust is that it evokes different expectations in different people who are disposed differently to trusting others and appreciating others' trust. From a managerial point of view, this is a matter of creating a shared sense of meaning while acknowledging and respecting peoples' different starting points. Again, this is not just a matter of getting people to buy into a particular theory of trust because it supposedly serves an organizational purpose. It is also a matter of cultural difference. A blind spot or limitation of the managerial literature on trust is that it tends to disregard such difference, thus assuming (if only implicitly) a certain cultural sameness and mutual identification among the parties involved in trusting relationships and exchanges. Hence, it has largely failed to consider issues regarding diversity and inequality. We do not claim to be able to correct this imbalance in this book, but we do address the resulting void of reflection in the coming chapters.

Trust, Social Capital and the Gift

The literature on organizational social capital arguably suffers from the same blindness to issues of diversity. We will address this problem in turn. However, we extend our argument regarding trust through the concept of social capital (see Chapter 4), and there are two basic reasons for this – one is theoretical, the other is practical/empirical. Not only are there obvious theoretical affinities between trust and social capital (when the starting point is a relational view of trust), "Social Capital" is also a well-established label for organizational efforts to build and support stronger intra- and interorganizational relations and collaboration. This is certainly the case among Danish public sector organizations.

Social capital is an often used measure of the relational value of trust. It signifies how trust can be an enabler of cooperation and relationship building within organizations (Tyler, 2003). Social capital is associated with high levels of collective goal orientation and shared trust, which can facilitate successful collective action (Leana & van Buren, 1999). Social capital makes it possible to work toward a valorization of trust and social relations as matters of value that can be spoken of in terms of capital (alongside other forms of capital). Social capital supports the insight that social norms are sometimes stronger than economic norms (Ariely, 2008). Moreover, different forms of social capital can serve to add some concreteness and structure to our understanding of what relational trust is or can be in organizational settings, covering both intra- and interorganizational relationships. Furthermore, we argue that the sociological and anthropological literature on gift exchange can serve to provide a fresh perspective on how social capital is created and maintained within modern organizations. Mauss (2000) has argued that, as part of a community, one is obliged to give, receive and reciprocate. This also applies to modern organizations, where social relationships and group boundaries are "formed and sustained through the perpetuating cycle of giving and receiving" (Dolfsma, Eijk & Jolink, 2009, p. 232). We pursue this idea and show how *the gift* has both prescriptive and explanatory value for an understanding of the workings of trust and social capital in public organizations.

That being said, the literature on organizational social capital, taken as a whole, is emblematic of the "optimistic bias" that also accrues to much trust scholarship. It tends to foreground positive aspects of human interaction and benevolent motivations for relationship building to the detriment of psychological and social/organizational barriers and constraints. Parallel to our double investment in "the relational", we need to reflect on the instrumental imperatives of the discourse on organizational social capital and how it can be supportive of a positive trust agenda, while also investigating its blind spots, exclusions and shortcomings (vis-à-vis its failure to consider issues of diversity).

A Relational Trust Agenda

Overall, our ambition in this book is to theorize the workings of trust in public sector organizations from the point of view of a reflexive sociology and with a particular eye for the explanatory value of a relational understanding of trust. In Chapter 2, we proceed to build our theoretical framework distinguishing between institutional, economic, moral and relational views of trust. We showcase not only the paradigmatic differences between the four views, but also how a dynamic understanding of the workings of organizational trust needs to account for their interconnectedness and the emergence of hybrid forms of governance and management that combine elements from different views. We then flesh out the properties of the relational view using relevant distinctions and insights from the trust literature. In Chapter 3, we show how a relational view of trust has affinities with (and needs to be seen in conjunction with) a relational view of power. We discuss how trust is related to control and to post-bureaucratic organizational developments and post-heroic leadership. We also dig into different forms of debureaucratization and provide a discussion of how the trust agenda relates to theories of motivation and motivation crowding. In Chapter 4, we relate trust to development in the scholarly literature on social capital in general and organizational social capital in particular. As indicated, we also touch on social exchange theory and how notions of the gift and gift exchange can serve to illuminate vital mechanisms in the creation, maintenance and development of organizational social capital. We also address matters of diversity and othering, and how social capital can help alleviate such concerns. In Chapter 5, we take a closer look at empirical cases illustrating different aspects of what makes or breaks intra- or interorganizational trust. Finally, in Chapter 6, we summarize our contribution and discuss future prospects of public sector trust development and future prospects for trust research focusing on this sector. Among the issues we touch on in the discussion of future prospects is technology and digitalization and how new digital solutions can play a part in addressing many of the problems that the trust agenda has brought up.

References

Adler, P. S. (2001). Market, hierarchy, and trust: The knowledge economy and the future of capitalism. *Organization Science*, 12(2), 215–234.

Argyris, C. & Schön, D. A. (1974). *Theory in practice: Increasing professional effectiveness.* San Francisco, CA: Jossey-bass.

Ariely, D. (2008). *Predictably irrational.* Great Britain: Harper.

Baier, A. (1986). Trust and antitrust. *Ethics*, 96(2), 231–260.

Bauman, Z. (1978). *Hermeneutics and social science: Approaches to Understanding.* London: Hutchinson.

Bijlsma-Frankema, K. & Costa, A. C. (2005). Understanding the trust-control nexus. *International Sociology*, 20(3), 259–282.

Bouckaert, G. (2012a). Reforming for performance and trust: Some reflections. *The NISPAcee Journal of Public Administration and Policy*, V(1), 9–20.

Bouckaert, G. (2012b). Trust and public administration. *Administration*, 60(1), 91–115.

Christensen, T. & Lægreid, P. (Eds.) (2007). *Transcending new public management: The transformation of public sector reforms.* Ashgate: Aldershot.

Christensen, T. & Lægreid, P. (2011). Complexity and hybrid public administration – theoretical and empirical challenges. *Public Organization Review*, 11(4), 407–423.

Clarke, J. & Newman, J. (1997). *The managerial state: Power, politics and ideology in the remaking of social welfare.* London: Sage Publications Ltd.

Costa, A. C. & Bijlsma-Frankema, K. (2007). Trust and control interrelations – New perspectives on the trust-control nexus. *Group & Organization Management* 32(4), 392–406.

Covey, S. & Link, G. (2013). *Smart trust.* New York, NY: Free Press.

Den danske regering. (2011). *Et Danmark, der står sammen. Regeringsgrundlag, oktober.* [A Denmark that stands together. Government plan] Downloaded from: www. stm.dk/publikationer/Et_Danmark_der_staar_sammen_11/Regeringsgrundlag_ okt_2011.pdf

Dolfsma, W., van der Eijk, R. & Jolink, A. (2009). On a source of social capital: Gift Exchange. *Journal of Business Ethics,* 89, 315–329.

Edelenbos, J. & Eshuis, J. (2012). The interplay between trust and control in governance processes: A conceptual and empirical investigation. *Administration & Society,* 44(6), 647–674.

European Commission, Directorate-General for Research and Innovation. (2017). *Trust at risk: Implications for EU policies and institutions.* Publications Office.

Fletcher, J. K. (2004). The paradox of postheroic leadership: An essay on gender, power, and transformational change. *The Leadership Quarterly,* 15(5), 647–661.

Fletcher, J. K. & Käufer, K. (2003). Shared leadership: Paradox and possibility. Ch. 2 in C. L. Pearce & J. A. Conger (Eds.). *Shared leadership: Reframing the hows and whys of leadership* (21–47). Thousand Oaks, CA: Sage.

Fukuyama, F. (1995). *Trust: The social virtues and the creation of prosperity.* England: Hamish Hamilton.

Gargiulo, M. & Ertug, G. (2006). The dark side of trust. In R. Bachmann & A. Zaheer (Eds.). *Handbook of trust research* (165–186). Cornwall: Edward Elgar.

Gergen, K. J. (1999). *An invitation to social construction.* Thousand Oaks, CA: Sage.

Ghoshal, S. (2005). Bad management theories are destroying good management practices. *Academy of Management Learning & Education,* 4(1), 75–91.

Giddens, A. (1984). *The constitution of society.* Oakland: University of California Press.

Gittell, J. H. (2006). Relational coordination: Coordinating work through relationships of shared goals, shared knowledge and mutual respect. In O. Kyriakidou & M. Ozbilgin (Eds.). *Relational perspectives in organizational studies: A research companion* (74–94). Northampton, MA: Edward Elgar.

Hartley, J. (2005). Innovation in governance and public services: Past and present. *Public Money & Management,* 25(1), 27–34.

Herold, P. (2019). *Trust, control and the economics of governance.* Oxon: Routledge.

Hood, C. & Dixon, R. (2015a). *A government that worked better and cost less? Evaluating three decades of reform and change in UK central government.* Oxford: Oxford University Press.

Hood, C. & Dixon, R. (2015b). What we have to show for 30 years of new public management: Higher costs, more complaints. *Governance: An International Journal of Policy, Administration and Institutions,* 28(3), 265–267.

Khodyakov, D. (2007). Trust as a process: A three-dimensional approach. *Sociology,* 41(1), 115–132.

Københavns Kommune. (2012). *Budget '13.* København: Københavns Kommune.

Københavns Kommune. (2015). *Budget '16.* København: Københavns Kommune.

Københavns Kommune. (2019). *Charter for arbejdsfællesskaber.* [Charter for work communities]. København: Økonomiforvaltningen.

Leana, C. R. & van Buren, H. J. (1999). Organizational social capital and employment practices. *Academy of Management Review,* 24(3), 538–555.

Luhmann, N. (2017). *Trust and power.* St. Ives: Polity Press.

Mauss, M. (2000). *The gift: Forms and functions of exchange in archaic societies.* New York: Norton.

Misztal, B. (1996). *Trust in modern societies: The search for the bases of social order.* Cornwall: Wiley.

Möllering, G. (2019). Connecting trust and power. *Journal of Trust Research*, 9(1), 1–5.

OECD. (2011). *The call for innovative and open government: An overview of country initiatives.* OECD Publishing, Paris.

OECD. (2017). *Trust and public policy: How better governance can help rebuild public trust.* OECD Public Governance Reviews, OECD Publishing, Paris.

Oomsels, P., Callens, M., Vanschoenwinkel, J. & Bouckaert, G. (2019). Functions and dysfunctions of interorganizational trust and distrust in the public sector. *Administration & Society*, 51(4), 516–544.

Osborne, S. P. (2006). The new public governance. *Public Management Review*, 8(3), 377–387.

Ospina, S. M. & Uhl-Bien, M. (2012). Introduction – Mapping the terrain. Convergence and divergence around relational leadership. In M. Uhl-Bien & S. M. Ospina (Eds.). *Advancing relational leadership. A dialogue among perspectives* (xix–xlxii). Charlotte, NC: Information Age Publishing.

Pearce, J. L. (2008). Bureaucracy and trust: A review of recent volumes in the Russell Sage Foundation Series on Trust. *International Public Management Journal*, 11(4), 481–485.

Pedersen, O. K. (2011). *Konkurrencestaten.* København: Hans Reitzels Forlag.

Plotnikof, M. (2016). Changing market values? Tensions of contradicting public management discourses. A case from the Danish daycare sector. *International Journal of Public Sector Management*, 29(7), 659–674.

Pollitt, C. & Bouckaert, G. (2011). *Public management reform: A comparative analysis – New public management, governance, and the neo–Weberian State*, 3rd edition. Oxford: Oxford University Press.

Pollitt, C. & Hupe, P. (2011). Talking about government. *Public Management Review*, 13(5), 641–658.

Regeringen, Akademikerne, Danske Regioner, FTF, KL & OAO. (2013). *Principper for samarbejde mellem parter på det offentlige arbejdsmarked om modernisering.* [Principles for collaboration between parties in the public labor market regarding modernization] Downloaded from www.kl.dk

Rousseau, D. M., Sitkin, S. B., Burt, R. S. & Camerer, C. (1998). Not so different after all: A cross-discipline view of trust. *Academy of Management Review* 23(3), 393–404.

Sheppard, B. H. & Sherman, D. M. (1998). The grammars of trust: A model and general implications. *The Academy of Management Review*, 23(3), 422–437.

Siltala, J. (2013). New public management: The evidence-based worst practice? *Administration & Society*, 45(4), 468–493.

Six, F. (2013). Trust in regulatory relations: How new insights from trust research improve regulation theory. *Public Management Review*, 15(2), 163–185.

Solomon, R. C. & Flores, F. (2001). *Building trust – in business, politics, relationships and life.* New York, NY: Oxford University Press.

Spillane, J. P. (2005). Distributed leadership. *The Educational Forum*, 69(2), 143–150.

Tyler, T. R. (2003). Trust within organisations. *Personnel Review*, 32(5), 556–568.

Vallentin, S. & Thygesen, N. (2017). Trust and control in public sector reform: Complementary and beyond. *Journal of Trust Research*, 7(2), 150–169.

Van de Walle, S. (2011). New public management: Restoring the public trust through creating distrust? In T. Christensen & P. Lægreid (Eds.). *Ashgate research companion to new public management* (309–320). Aldershot: Ashgate.

Wacquant, L. J. D. (1992). Toward a social praxeology: The structure and logic of Bourdieu's sociology. In P. Bourdieu & L. J. D. Wacquant (Eds.). *An invitation to reflexive sociology* (1–59). Oxford: Polity Press.

Weziak-Bialowolska, D. & Dijkstra, L. (2015). *Trust, local governance and quality of public service in EU regions and cities*. EUR 27195. Luxembourg: Publications Office of the European Union, JRC92655.

2 Trust Paradigms in Public Management

There is a tendency for the scholarly literature on trust and management to invest little effort in defining and reflecting more rigorously on the concept of trust itself. In fact, there has been surprisingly little interaction between the scholarly literature on trust and the management literature (Jagd, 2009). We want to make a contribution toward remedying this state of affairs and consider the scholarly literature as an important resource for our understanding of public management and governance. Fortunately, in speaking about the prevalence of different public trust paradigms, we do find prior research contributions that serve to build bridges between trust literature and public administration research. Thus, we are not the first to suggest that there are different basic understandings of trust at play in different notions of public management and governance and that the scholarly trust literature is useful for showcasing and giving some theoretical backbone to this insight. In making this argument, we build on prior research by Bouckaert (2012a, 2012b) and Van de Walle (2011, 2017) in particular. Overall, we present a novel framework for understanding the different faces of trust in public administration, with part of the novelty being attributable to our strong emphasis on the workings of relational and thus social trust. It is an area that arguably calls for more sustained reflection.

Bouckaert (2012a) provides a productive starting point for this endeavor. He takes his point of departure in the seminal paper by Rousseau et al. (1998), who distinguish between four types of trust: (1) *deterrence-based trust*, which suggests that for another to be trustworthy there needs to be effective sanctions in place to punish aberrant or opportunistic behavior; (2) *calculus-based trust*, which is an embodiment of rational choice and modeled on interactions based on economic exchange. According to Rousseau et al. (1998), this type of trust derives not only from the existence of deterrence, but also from information about the other, including signals such as reputation and certification; (3) *relational trust*, which derives from repeated interactions over time between trustor and trustee. The basis of relational trust is formed by information available to trustors and trustees from within the relationship itself. Being reliable and dependable in repeated interactions with the trustor can thus give rise to positive expectations about the intentions and qualifications of the trustee; (4) *institution-based trust*, which refers to the

DOI: 10.4324/9780429431104-2

trust effects of institutions ranging from legal systems to social and cultural norms – and the latent or manifest sanctions associated with the breach of rules or norms (Rousseau et al., 1998). Institution-based trust can both be seen as a control mechanism (a deterrent against opportunism) and as a form of trust support (cf. Shapiro, 1987). We return to this issue below and in our treatment of the trust-control nexus (see Chapter 3).

Rousseau et al. (1998) conclude that deterrence-based trust, with its focus on control mechanisms and sanctions, is not really trust after all, and therefore end up excluding it from their trust framework. However, we cannot take deterrence out of the trust equation entirely. Deterrence plays a role in the constitution of both calculus- and institution-based trust and thus reenters our theoretical framing. Along the same lines, Lewicki and Bunker (1996) (citing Shapiro, Sheppard & Cheraskin, 1992) argue that calculus-based trust *is* deterrence-based trust – that is, a form of trust preoccupied with assuring consistency of behavior by making sure that individuals are fearful of not living up to agreements and promises made. Trust is sustained to the extent that the deterrent (punishment, sanction) is clearly articulated and likely to occur if trust is violated. However, according to Lewicki and Bunker (1996), calculus-based trust is *not only* preoccupied with deterrence and fear of punishment for violating trust, it is also concerned with the rewards that can be derived from preserving it. As they put it, "trust is an ongoing, market-oriented, economic calculation whose value is derived by determining the outcomes resulting from creating and sustaining the relationship relative to the costs of maintaining or severing it" (p. 120). In other words, trust is considered within a utilitarian market/cost-benefit/rational choice logic. They still insist, though, that the negative deterrence elements will be more dominant motivators than the positive benefit-seeking elements. While we largely agree with this point, we will put a different spin on it in our theoretical framework (see below). In sum, we will not use deterrence-based trust as a stand-alone category in our theoretical framework, but we will strongly emphasize the significance of deterrence in the constitution of calculus-based *and* institution-based trust.

What about the constitution of relational trust, then? According to Rousseau et al. (1998), this is where emotions enter the fray as frequent, longer-term interactions can lead to reciprocated interpersonal care and concern among the involved parties. Relational trust can thus be considered as *affective trust* (McAllister, 1995) or *identity-based trust* (Coleman, 1990). According to Lewicki and Bunker (1996), identity- or identification-based trust "develops as one both knows and predicts the other's needs, choices, and preferences and also shares some of those same needs, choices and preferences as one's own" (p. 123). It involves a mutual understanding and appreciation of other's desires, needs or intentions.

Lewicki and Bunker (1996) present a framework distinguishing between calculus-based trust, knowledge-based trust and identification-based trust. Van de Walle's (2017) application of this framework to trust relations in the public sector is an illustrative example of the importance of distinctions – as they set boundary conditions for how we attribute meaning and value to different types of trust. According to Van de Walle, it is contractual relationships, performance-related rewards and punishments, including public naming and shaming, that allow calculus-based trust to develop, whereas knowledge-based trust relies on information about the other and implies that knowledge, openness and transparency can support predictability of interactions and other's actions – both internally (T3) and in relations to citizens (T1 and T2). Finally, he associates identification-based trust with perceptions of shared values and mutual identification. Importantly, Van de Walle (2017) argues that this type of trust – in contrast to the other two – is mainly emotional rather than cognitive and, for each individual, is limited to just a few relationships (in particular ones based on shared sociopolitical, ethnic or political values and backgrounds).

Its merits notwithstanding, Lewicki and Bunker's framework, or perhaps rather Van de Walle's application of it, provides a narrow and limiting interpretation of institutional as well as relational trust (in the guise of identification-based trust). With regard to the former, we will argue that institutional trust has much broader application and bandwidth in this setting than provision of knowledge supporting transparency and predictable and supposedly rational outcomes. With regard to the latter, we will argue that relational trust is about much more than close personal relationships in organizations. In Van de Walle's conception, it has limited application only; in ours, it refers more broadly to developments in public sector management and governance. A key point in our conceptualization is that there is more to "the relational" than emotional attachments and that it cannot be contained within categories such as identification-based or affective trust. To fully capture these important facets of trust, we need to introduce an additional category: *moral trust*.

Thus, for present purposes (and in accordance with Bouckaert, 2012a), we find that the framework of Rousseau et al. (1998) provides a more productive basis for conceptualizing trust in public management. Before getting to that, however, we need to address the question of how we fundamentally define trust. Rousseau et al. (1998), and many before and after them, have defined trust as a psychological state and argued that this is a productive starting point for theory building and for building bridges between scholarly disciplines. But, as they also argue, "trust is at once related to dispositions, decisions, behaviors, social networks and institutions" (p. 394). The psychological starting point is symptomatic of how the trust literature often starts with the individual and/or dyadic relations. But there are other options.

Instead of conceptualizing trust as a psychological event within the individual, we approach it as a multidimensional social reality and a property of collective units. Trust is thus applicable to relations among people rather than individual psychological states (Lewis & Weigert, 1985). Following Lewis and Weigert (1985, p. 969), we argue "that the primary function of trust is sociological rather than psychological, since individuals would have no occasion or need to trust apart from social relationships". In the words of Luhmann (2017, p. 7), "trust is a social relationship which is subject as such to its own rules. Trust occurs within a framework of interaction which is influenced by both psychic and social systems, and cannot be exclusively associated with either." Trust thus sits at the boundary of sociology and psychology (Tyler, 2003). Our insistence on the primacy of the social and relational nature of trust has a number of implications, one being a focus on social action and thus behavioral enactment of trust (Lewis & Weigert, 1985). Trust, in this view, is not reducible to thinking or feeling; it is about *doing* and *saying* and what happens when people act and communicate in certain ways in social settings. And it is about institutions and systems as impersonal carriers of trust, giving primacy to structure over individual agency.

Speaking of trust as a property of collective units and as a multidimensional social reality provides us with, as outlined in Chapter 1, a basis for theorizing different perspectives on trust, their underlying assumptions and social implications. The reflexive sociological lens allows us to see how the basic forms of trust are embedded in particular ways in the history and development of public management and governance. And it allows us to reflect on the various ways in which trust is subjected to theories and practices of management and governance. Alas, instead of trying to understand or explain what makes or breaks trust at the individual level, we want to understand how trust is woven into the ways and means of public management and governance. As we have argued, a relational approach opens up to a broader theoretical engagement with trust as an organizational phenomenon – without cutting the ties to the scholarly trust literature (as is often the case with the popular managerial literature on trust). We now proceed to build our framework for understanding trust as part of the multidimensional social reality that is the modern public sector.

Trust Paradigms

We distinguish between four paradigmatic understandings of trust as a social phenomenon. To provide a systematic account of key properties and differences and similarities between the different perspectives, we have placed them in the two by two matrix below.

On one axis, we distinguish between trust as a (structural) background variable as opposed to trust as part of social interactions – what social actors

Table 2.1 Trust paradigms

	Social structures and processes	*Fundamental assumptions and principles*
Trust as background (system trust)	**INSTITUTIONAL**	**ECONOMIC**
Trust as foreground (social trust)	**RELATIONAL**	**MORAL**

do and their relationships with one another. In other words, we distinguish between understandings that put emphasis on (impersonal) system trust and understandings that emphasize the significance of social trust (between people). When the focus is on system trust (Luhmann, 2017), trust becomes a background variable, whereas a focus on social trust means that trust is foregrounded as a more tangible managerial concern.

On the other axis, we distinguish between trust as a product of social structures and processes, as distinct from more fundamental assumptions and principles. The former makes trust an empirical and thus variable question, embedded in a certain place and time. Institutional framework conditions can both enable and inhibit trust, and it is bound to differ how managers deal with trust and how it works in social relations. As we will show, the institutional and relational understandings embody both variation and ambiguity. Conversely, the economic and moral understandings of trust build on strong assumptions – negative and positive respectively – about human nature and what motivates people. These assumptions are normative and principled in the sense that they are not open to empirical correction. They are what they are. In this sense, they are localised outside of specific spatial and temporal coordinates and therefore are more "fundamental". We will now take a closer look at the institutional paradigm as a manifestation of system trust.

Institutional Trust

Institutional understandings of trust stress the importance of rules and norms that are largely taken for granted within organizations, particular institutional fields or society as a whole (Zucker, 1986). Trust is associated with entrenched – formal and informal – ways of doing things that are not usually questioned or challenged. Trust is thus a background variable, requiring no further explanation, independent thought or action. It belongs to the realm of the familiar and the routine (Möllering, 2006). People trust because they experience that others trust too (Luhmann, 2017). In the public sector, this perspective is closely associated with the classical model of governance, with its focus on formal rules, procedures and sanctions, and its hierarchical allocation of roles (posts), competencies and responsibility. In the classical, ideal type Weberian bureaucracy, there is no need to talk explicitly about trust, as it is embedded in organizational structures and professional norms (Grey & Garsten, 2001).

Institutional trust ideally stems from the system working the way it is supposed to work – as a means of guaranteeing impersonal and disinterested (and therefore fair) treatment and allocation of rights and duties, without discrimination or corruption. Meritocracy, universalism and neutrality serving as core bureaucratic values (Monteiro & Adler, 2022). According to Weber, the ideal type public bureaucracy is an embodiment of instrumental rationality supported by legally legitimated authority. The ends of action are determined by those at the top of the hierarchy of authority, while the task of subordinates is to pursue the most rational and efficient ways to realize those ends (ibid.).

Under such circumstances, trust "is not understood as an attribute of individuals (their 'trustworthiness') but is, rather, an artefact of following rules of conduct. Trust is therefore installed within organizational routines and it is these which bestow predictability and reliability" (Grey & Garsten, 2001, p. 234). Trust becomes a nonissue due to highly formalized rules and interactions (Van de Walle, 2011). This insight applies more broadly to modern organizations, where we "find impersonal trust embedded in the hierarchy of authority and role expectations, particularly in the expectation of technically competent role performance" (Choudhury, 2008, p. 596). Bureaucratization of trust is thus taken to mean its embeddedness in organizational rules, norms, structures, routines – and subsequent non-reliance upon the subjective assessments of trustors and trustees. Thus, this perspective on trust puts emphasis on the significance of (especially formal) organizational rules and norms, including policies, models of governance, forms of management and other systems and technologies through which work is organized. That is to say, trust is attributed to established social structures rather than the social actions of individuals and interpersonal relationships. Institutional trust plays an import role not least in large and fragmented organizations characterized by considerable spatial and social distances. It can serve to build bridges and create a common ground among actors unfamiliar with each other (Oomsels & Bouckaert, 2014).

We can refer to this as a form of system trust. In the trust literature, there is some disagreement as to whether it should be regarded as trust at all, or whether it is more readily associable with control and deterrence. Keeping in mind the three perspectives on the public sector and trust, T1 is mainly reliant upon institutional and thus impersonal trust. In the words of Pearce (2008, p. 482), "public managers and policy makers produce trust through the establishment and maintenance of organizations enforcing and administering the rule of law, citizens' trust in contracts, and in one another". It is organizational structures, processes, rules and contracts that matter, not (corruptible) social relationships. The ideal type public bureaucracy can thus be considered as a form of *organized distrust* – in the specific sense that it has a built-in non-reliance upon social trust. This non-reliance can even be considered a virtue, as it is meant to curtail corruption and unequal treatment while supporting transparency and accountability.

We do not question the material significance and primacy of control and deterrence with regard to T1 relationships. However, there is more to institutional trust than these functions. On the one hand, institutional trust is, generally speaking, an embodiment of how trust is attributable to system elements rather than social relationships. On the other, there is the more specific matter of how trust can be made subject to public management and governance at the level of T3 relationships. This opens up to greater variability and different potentials and outcomes. Institutional trust can be supportive of bureaucratic as well as economic and post-bureaucratic developments in management and governance. Vis-à-vis the assumptions and prescriptions of New Public Governance (NPG), it is not a given that institutional mechanisms need to be all about (latent or manifest) sanctions and avoiding negative outcomes and cannot also provide positive support for social trust.

Analytically, we consider system trust as an important complement to social trust because it helps provide a broader scope for the discussion of trust in public organizations. The institutional perspective reminds us that calls for social and relational trust need to be considered in context and against the backdrop of institutional constraints and enablers – that is, in relation to the systemic conditions and requirements that prevail in the public sector in general and in particular public organizations: the tasks that need to be carried out, the public services that must be delivered, binding rules and regulations, budgets, rights of citizens. Besides, systemic problems call for systemic solutions. To the extent that public sector organizations are subject to rampant economization, bureaucratic rule-following and lack of trust, we should not expect that such problems can be properly addressed or overcome from the bottom and up, via appeal to middle managers and employees experiencing the importance of relational trust on a daily basis. It is also necessary to address institutional change processes, including new forms of management and governance, or new uses/interpretations of existing models, and the impacts that these can have on trust in public organizations. To iterate, trust reform processes in the Scandinavian countries are examples of how experiments can be made with the management and governance of trust, with the aim of providing systemic support for social trust and associated benefits (see Chapter 5).

Economic Trust

Economic trust designates the realm of calculus-based trust, meaning that trust is considered within a utilitarian market/cost-benefit/rational choice logic. Quoting, once again, Lewicki and Bunker (1996, p. 120), "trust is an ongoing, market-oriented, economic calculation whose value is derived by determining the outcomes resulting from creating and sustaining the relationship relative to the costs of maintaining or severing it". The tendency for economic theory to turn trust into a background variable is well articulated by Dasgupta (1988, p. 49), who writes: "Trust is central to all transactions and yet economists rarely discuss the notion. It is treated rather as a *background environment*, present whenever called upon, a sort of ever-ready lubricant that permits voluntary participation in production and exchange" (our emphasis). The ideal market, as imagined by neoclassical economics, is characterized by "perfect information and pure competition between independent and faceless trades, [and] does not involve trust as a central concept, since the competitive market is supposed to control any deception" (Blomqvist, 1997, p. 274). Furthermore, rational choice theory excludes differences among economic actors, which means that none are considered more trustworthy than others (ibid.).

Although economic approaches, as already mentioned, are not oblivious to the enabling benefits of trust, we concur with Lewicki and Bunker's interpretation that deterrence elements feature most prominently in the economic understanding of trust (see also Möllering, 2006). It is first and foremost about avoiding negative outcomes. Hence, the starting point is a set of negative assumptions about human behavior and motivation. It is an understanding that is based on neoclassical economy theory and which evokes its pivotal actor/agent: the rational and self-interested homo economicus. Opportunism and antagonistic interests are central concerns. How best to protect oneself from the potentially damaging actions of the opportunistic other? According to Casson and Della Giusta (2006):

> The need for trust in neoclassical economic theory stems from the impossibility of monitoring other people's behavior, and the fact that the selfish individuals who cannot be monitored are aware of this, and recognize the opportunity it affords to cheat the other party. The solution is to devise enforceable contracts which modify incentives and thereby induce selfish people to behave in a socially responsible way.
>
> (p. 340)

The basic idea is that trust – as a scarce, intangible resource – is justified if or when the other party has little or no inclination to violate trust due to effective sanctions being in place – sanctions that are preferably outlined in formal contracts. It is often argued that (smart) trust reduces transaction costs and may even in some instances be a more effective way to reduce transaction costs than formal contracts. Focusing on signals such as reputation and certification and on continued encounters between contracting parties are examples of this (vis-à-vis the notion of *relational* contracting). However, economic scholarship has arguably failed to fully embrace this possibility and to provide a convincing explanation for how economic actors can assess each other's behavior as trustworthy to begin with and handle the involved uncertainties and vulnerabilities without legal safeguards in place. The economic concept of trust is thus reminiscent of distrust. That is, distrust – aiming to exert control over the (opportunistic) other and make future outcomes predictable – becomes a prerequisite for trust, albeit trust in a limited calculative and transactional form. Hence, Oliver Williamson, the father of transaction cost economics, has argued that noncalculative trust is irrelevant for economic exchange and should be reserved for personal relations only (Williamson, 1993). Although Williamson has acknowledged that managers often act on the basis of trust, he finds that the difficulty of identifying trustworthy agents is so great that organizations are better off acting and structuring themselves as if all agents are untrustworthy (Hosmer, 1995).

While institutional trust has a large bandwidth (it can be supportive of economic as well as relational trust), economic trust has a narrower scope.

Being a systemic form of trust, its favored vehicles are contracts and output- and performance-based models of management and governance – supported by systems of quantification, measurement, surveillance, control and compliance. Speaking of public management and governance more specifically, economic trust is embodied in New Public Management (NPM) and public choice thinking. Public choice is based on the idea that self-interested public officials cannot be trusted. It comes with a skeptical or cynical view of the public sector ethos and articulates a moral economy of distrust. Moreover, NPM differs from other governance archetypes, in particular the Weberian assumption of public officials acting in accordance with the public interest, in making distrust the basic condition for collaboration in the public sector. Distrust among antagonistic actors – principals and agents – is assumed to prevail at all levels (Van de Walle, 2011). Hence, orthodox principal-agent theory, and orthodox applications of its insights, predicts the absence and unsustainability of trust (Möllering, 2006; Sheppard & Sherman, 1998).

These assumptions lead directly to an idealization of marketization, privatization, economic incentives and competition as key drivers of public sector development. Marketization of trust is thus taken to mean its embeddedness in market-like arrangements favoring atomistic and short-term contractual relations (tit for tat) over more long-term social relations involving mutual commitment and reciprocity beyond the bare minimum among the involved parties. NPM ascribes particular material significance and thus primacy to economic measures of worth and success, to the detriment of other, less quantifiable and measurable markers. The prescribed market-based disaggregation of the public sector into autonomous units in continuous competition with each other can in turn lead to decline with regard to cohesion, common values and collaboration (Van de Walle, 2011). However, one thing is assumptions, another is social outcomes. If the calculus-based approach worked as intended, other forms of trust would be superfluous as the principal would be able to predict with great certainty the actions of the agent. But, such rationalistic attempts to predict and control desired behavior do not, as a rule, work as intended. Economic incentives do not guarantee desired outcomes, which is to say that trust is needed even in contractual relationships (Fox, 1974; Lane, 2000). In the words of Luhmann (1979, p. 25): "Despite every effort of organization and rational planning, it is impossible for all actions to be guided by means of reliable forecasts of their consequences. There are leftover uncertainties to be accommodated …" In social exchange and economic transactions, risks of aberrant or opportunistic behavior are unavoidable, and a calculated, transactional approach is not necessarily the best way to address this problem of "leftover uncertainties". Hence, distrust can turn out to be a self-fulfilling prophecy: if you meet others with calculated distrust, you will usually be treated in kind, and this precludes any opportunity to benefit from the advantages associated with a trust-based relationship.

To iterate, NPM is based on a simplified and negative view of human nature and what motivates people. This can in turn have performative effects through the mechanism of the self-fulfilling prophecy. Mindsets and behaviors in the organization can, for better or worse, come to emulate the theoretical model when economic assumptions are built into management practices, institutional arrangements, language and social norms (Ferraro, Pfeffer & Sutton, 2005). This again points to the notion of the double hermeneutic that we touched upon in Chapter 1. It does not suffice to criticize NPM for being out of touch with the social reality and individual experiences and preferences in public organizations. We also need to be aware of how the theory and practice of NPM partake in creating this very reality and the impact this has on performance, motivation and well-being. As an embodiment of economic trust, NPM ascribes trust to contracts and economic forms of management and governance. It tends to be preoccupied with quantification and measurement as calculative enablers of streamlining, cost cutting, effectiveness and transparency. Moral trust is in many ways the polar opposite to economic trust and NPM.

Moral Trust

The institutional and the economic trust paradigm represent the dominant views of public sector organization: the rule- and norms-based Weberian or neo-Weberian bureaucracy and the economizing force of NPM. Moral and relational trust constitute alternatives or complements to these established models and place trust in the foreground of managerial consideration. Within the moral paradigm, trust is considered as a fundamental human value or virtue and a normative demand levelled at individual human beings. Trusting relations are seen to constitute a particular form of moral community (Uslaner, 2002) or moral bond (Sztompka, 2019). Moral trust stands in sharp contrast to the calculated instrumentalism of economic trust as it replaces negative assumptions with equally strong positive assumptions about human behavior and motivation.

Underneath the variable repertoire of epistemic reasons for showing trust, there is a more deeply set moral ontology (cf. Cohen & Dienhart, 2013). This is one way to convey the essence of the moral trust argument. Trust establishes a moral relationship and involves a moral commitment. Therefore, theories that emphasize strategic behavior, rational decision making and cost/benefit calculation are inadequate (ibid.). They are inadequate because they obscure "the moral nature of trust and also the presence of substantive obligation in trust relationships, rather than mere expectations or beliefs held by the trusting party" (Cohen & Dienhart, 2013, p. 9). However, there is another way to convey the argument; one that is somewhat less ontological and puts greater emphasis on moral choice and agency. As Lagerspetz (1998) articulates it, based on the work of Levinas and Løgstrup (see below), the moral nature of trust is not a psychological discovery or an empirical phenomenon whose existence can be established in a "neutral" manner. Moral trust is "a way of *looking* at things" (Lagerspetz, 1998, p. 163) that involves an urge "to view human interaction in *a certain light*" (ibid., p. 162). You are not compelled by logic to adopt it, neither can it be forced upon you, but you can choose to consider (or simply consider) human relations as moral bonds and thus commit yourself to trust as a moral principle.

Moral trust can be described in terms of affective trust and identification-based trust. It does tend to favor emotions over cognition in the sense that trust, reflected in good will and benevolence toward others, is considered as a foundational and natural starting point for human coexistence and therefore requires no rational justification. Moral trust is not necessarily irrational, but it defies rational assessment criteria. Trust as a moral and existential imperative is perhaps most clearly articulated in the work of the Danish ethical philosopher and theologian Knud E. Løgstrup. Løgstrup (1997) writes:

> It is characteristic of human life that we normally encounter one another with natural trust. This is true not only in the case of persons who are well acquainted with one another but also in the case of complete strangers. (…) Initially we believe one another's word; initially we trust each other. This may indeed seem strange, but it is a part of what it means to be human. Human life could hardly exist if it were otherwise. We would simply not be able to live; our life would be impaired and wither away if we were in advance to distrust one another, if we were to suspect the other of thievery and falsehood from the very outset.
>
> (pp. 8–9)

According to Løgstrup (1997), trust and distrust are not equal ways of being. Trust is basic, distrust merely designates the absence of trust. It is the "deficient form" of trust. Trust is reflective of deep-seated human values and social inclinations and represents an unconditional human and social good. The natural thing is to meet others with good will, openness, positive expectations, benevolence, empathy (vis-à-vis identification-based trust). This is not to say, however, that trust needs to be unconditional in practice. To trust, Løgstrup writes, is to lay oneself open, which is why we tend to react with great vehemence when our trust is abused. While he considers trust and the self-surrender that goes with it as basic facts of human life, he also acknowledges the workings of, if you will, disenchanted social worlds wherein people trust one another with great reservation, hold themselves in reserve and do not allow themselves to trust completely (Løgstrup, 1997). This description is arguably more reminiscent of modern organizations.

However, the moral point remains: trust comes first, distrust (and variations on this theme) second. Trust is the natural and positive starting point. This view finds support in popular management literature espousing trust as a managerial virtue and value. More importantly, for our purposes, moral trust is reflected in the actions, decisions and presence of public sector managers whose leadership is characterized by strong values. Trust-based leadership is arguably strongest and most authentic when practiced by managers who do it just because that is how they do things – in a non-contrived way that transcends calculation – beyond management fads and fashions, beyond the language and practices of trust reform. If it is not always the case that action speaks louder than words, it is certainly the case with trust. Following Løgstrup (1997), the demand (regarding trust), which is present in any human relationship, is tacit and thus unspoken (Lagerspetz, 1998). It is also radical, meaning that it arises out of the fact that in a social relation one person is delivered over into the hands of another person, yet

> The demand gives no directions whatever about how the life of the person thus delivered is to be taken care of. It specifies nothing in this respect but leaves it entirely to the individual. To be sure, the other person is to be served through word and action, but precisely which word and which action we must ourselves decide in each situation. And we must learn this from our own unselfishness and our own understanding of life.
>
> (Løgstrup, 1997, p. 56)

This argument is akin to an ethics of proximity, defying rules and social norms and attributing responsibility solely to the individual (Bevan & Corvellec, 2007). Or perhaps more accurately, throwing responsibility back on the individual.

While we acknowledge the importance of moral trust, we also want to point to its limitations and how it differs from relational trust. Moral trust, as we have presented it, embodies a strong and demanding management philosophy that, apart from providing idealized prescriptions, arguably resonates with the common sense and real-life experiences of many modern managers. However, it fails to provide a more elaborate account of the context in which trusting (or distrusting) relationship is embedded, and it does tend to have special appeal for managers with a special disposition for trust, whether this is taken to mean a values-based or existential approach to leadership. Although such leadership is an important resource for development of organizational trust, it fails to provide a vantage point for understanding and synthesizing the different understandings of trust that prevail in public organizations.

For that, we will argue, we have to turn to relational trust and be less preoccupied with the individual as moral arbiter and explanatory starting point. Prior public administration research has tended to conflate moral and relational trust in the sense that relational trust has been closely affiliated with affective underpinnings of trust. Unlike institutional and economic trust, relational trust has been construed as a matter of emotion rather than cognition. As a result, institutional and economic trust have gained the cognitive and rational upper hand, lending further support to the intellectual bias against social trust. We want to correct this state of affairs and argue for the cognitive value and material significance of relational trust as a complement to institutional trust and a corrective and/or alternative to economic trust. We will also show how relational trust is able to appreciate but nevertheless differs from moral trust in that it emphasizes the social conditioning of trust and attributes greater variability and ambiguity to trust. We will show how relational trust is part and parcel of spoken demands and concerns regarding management, governance, power and control in the public sector. Relational trust houses weaker assumptions about the positive worth of trust, but provides a stronger basis for understanding and promoting trust in a public sector context. This is, in a nutshell, our argument regarding social trust.

Relational Trust

The relational paradigm, then, is reflective of a sociological investment in trust. The focus is on social relationships instead of the individual, its disposition or psyche. Instead of strong assumptions supporting the positive value of social trust, we get a more tempered or balanced approach aiming to capture the pros and cons and ambivalence of social trust. Instead of trust as an unconditional and unspoken moral demand, we get conditional and experience-based trust. Instead of moral principles and emotions, we get an integrated, material and cognitive view of trust, power, control and value creation.

With regard to how relational trust differs from institutional and economic trust, the simple and stereotypical explanation is that they represent different points of view with vested interests and priorities. Institutional and economic trust are associable with the top-down (higher level) view of political leadership, top management and centralized planning and budgeting. From the top-down point of view, irregularities are often best handled through the knee-jerk reaction of regulation: new rules, command and control. And economic governance, as we have seen, is not prone to valorize or appreciate the benefits of social trust. From the bottom-up (lower level) point of view, social trust tends to appear much more pressing and significant. Middle managers and employees are closer to the action, to the carrying out of operational tasks, and they are directly exposed to the actual consequences of political and managerial decisions and the impact they can have on trust relations in the organization. Whereas social trust – manager-manager, manager-employee, employee-employee, trust culture – may seem like a remote concern from the top-down perspective, it is bound to be a much more salient and material concern when considered bottom-up. It is a matter of social distance versus proximity. At a distance, looking down at the organization from way up the hierarchical ladder, social trust may seem like a risky, brittle and somewhat suspicious proposition. In the thick of managerial action, closer to the ground and operations, it can appear to be an absolute necessity.

However, we should not take this division for granted. It is not a given that the top-down perspective is all about bureaucratic rules and market norms to the detriment of social trust and social norms. Developments in NPG and post-bureaucratic organizational thinking (see Chapter 3) are reflective of how relational insights are being incorporated into institutional designs, governance and planning. Hence, it is misleading to assume that system trust belongs to the realm of governance while social trust is a feature of management. Social trust can be subject to governance, and system trust can, for better or worse, have deep imprints on managerial practices.

One of the strengths of relational trust, as we conceive it, is that it is able to capture a particular way of understanding and acting on trust, alongside certain normative ideals, while also providing a vantage point for understanding how different understandings of trust interconnect and affect one another in theory and practice. Speaking of interconnectedness, we want to provide an account that avoids institutional overdetermination as well as institutional underdetermination of social practices. As pointed out by Choudhury (2008, p. 596), relational trust can be embedded in structural conditions, "but is also enacted through individual or organizational behaviour in a given situation". To speak of relational trust is to foreground trust as a tangible managerial issue and concern. It is to put emphasis on prospects of managerial agency and action, but we have to consider this is in terms of situated agency, both with regard to internal and external environments. Organizational context is, directly and indirectly, formally and informally, related to the generation and maintenance of relational trust. The question is, then, how, given particular institutional constraints and enablers, organizations can devise structures and promote behavior to support relational trust (Six & Sorge, 2008).

Speaking of relational trust, then, is to acknowledge the importance of leadership without being overly preoccupied with individual dispositions in general and uniquely equipped – values-based, transformational, authentic, supposedly trustworthy – leaders in particular. Instead of invariant moral principles, the relational perspective considers trust as a continuous and dynamic process of learning and development involving managers and employees. Instead of gravitating toward individualized managerial manifestations of trust (leading by example etc.), we maintain a focus on trust as a social, relational, organizational matter. We are less preoccupied with relational trust as a particular way for individuals to experience trust and more with its entanglement in other parts of social reality, including how trust can act as a governance mechanism. Thus, we want to show how relational trust is related to notions of relational power and relational organization, social capital and post-bureaucratic organizational developments and potentials more broadly.

Trust Paradigms, Models of Public Governance and Hybrid Forms

We can now summarize our outline of the different paradigms in an expanded matrix.

Furthermore, we can summarize how the four paradigms are aligned with the dominant archetypes of public sector governance.

As mentioned, the institutional and the economic paradigm undoubtedly constitute the dominant views of public sector management and governance. We can thus reformulate our claim that there is an intellectual bias against

Table 2.2 Trust paradigms – Expanded matrix

	Social structures and processes	*Fundamental assumptions and principles*
Trust as background (system trust)	**Institutional trust** Structures, rules, norms Bureaucratization Sanctions, rewards	**Economic trust** Opportunism, self-interest Marketization Contracts, deterrence
Trust as foreground (social trust)	**Relational trust** Processes, actors Social relations, social capital Conditional, becoming	**Moral trust** Good will, benevolence Virtue, moral value Unconditional, being

Table 2.3 Trust paradigms and models of public governance

INSTITUTIONAL	**The Classical or Neo-Weberian Model** • Bureaucracy • Profession
ECONOMIC	**New Public Management** • Market • Contract
MORAL	(public service motivation, bureaucratic or public ethos, values-based management, managerial virtues)
RELATIONAL	**New Public Governance** • Self-management, self-governance • The relational organization

trust in political science and economics: these disciplines have a preference for system trust and bureaucratization or marketization narratives over social trust. They are not blind to the value and significance of trust, but tend to reduce it to a background variable. Now, the workings of moral and relational trust should be considered not in splendid isolation, but as correctives and/or complements to the other two. They are not full-blown alternatives, but to some extent embedded within institutional and economic framework conditions. Supporting a relational understanding, Adler (2001) speaks of how, alongside hierarchy (authority) and market (prize) as ideal-typical organizational forms, there is a third form, community, that relies on trust as coordinating mechanism. One function of trust is to mitigate weaknesses of hierarchy and market. Thus, trust complements authority and prize with norms of reciprocity, benevolence, mutual commitment and goodwill (see Chapter 4 on social capital). As he points out, modern trust is never blind trust, but reflective and conditional trust, built up through social interactions and social experiences involving different social actors (Adler, 2001). You cannot replace institutional requirements with relational trust or individualized moral demands, but you can recognize the value and significance of one or both for the workings of public organizations. The overall relational point is that we need to have an eye for the dynamic interplay between the different views and their organizational manifestations.

To iterate, institutional trust has close affiliations with the classical Weberian model of bureaucracy and the neo-Weberian state, where support for core Weberian values goes hand in with moderate reform initiatives (Pollitt & Bouckaert, 2011). Economic trust finds its purest expression in NPM, whereas relational trust is reflected in developments in NPG. Moral trust is a more diffuse entity with regard to governance, but can be related to Weberian notions of value rationality and a bureaucratic ethos rooted in expertise, professional discretion and a sense of calling (Monteiro & Adler, 2022). It has affinities with developments in values-based management, managerial virtues and similar perspectives within the realm of management philosophy. Besides, we can relate it to the notion of *public service motivation* (PSM) and thus an understanding of public sector employees as altruists with "warm hands" who are driven by a motivation to serve citizens, society and the common good to the best of their ability (see Chapter 3). This in turn evokes the notion of a *public sector ethos*, that is, the idea that there are norms, values and arrangements that are particular to the public sector and to the provision of public service, and which are not reducible to economic calculation and instrumentalism.

Speaking of citizens and society, the four models harbor different understandings of citizens, clients, patients, users. The institutional perspective considers the citizen as a *carrier of rights and duties*, whereas the economic perspective sees a *consumer* who preferably should be given a right to choose between different service offerings within a market setting. The moral perspective is bound to consider the citizen as an *individual with particular needs*, while the relational perspective sees a potential and resourceful *collaborator*.

To iterate, the trust paradigms with their allegiances to different models of governance should not be considered as static and separate entities. Ideal or pure types are helpful in elucidating vital differences and clarifying rules of engagement between different understandings of trust. Beyond that, we need to explore their dynamic interactions and the practical possibility of hybrid forms combining elements from different paradigms. For example, we should not assume beforehand that NPM, in practice, is a total stranger to (social) trust, as some practical efforts to support trust involve continued use of tools from the NPM toolbox (see Chapter 5). This in turn points to the need for us to reflect on the intricate relationships between trust, power and control (see Chapter 3). In practice, governance models can make use of insights from different trust paradigms and are thus not locked into particular relationships. Again, we find instances of NPM-based governance being justified with prescriptions taken from the relational model. The ways in which public organizations approach and work with trust will often combine/contain elements from more or all the mentioned paradigms. This allows us, again, to speak of hybrid forms of trust-based management.

In sum, Tables 2.2 and 2.3 provide us with an overview of ideal or pure types of trust and how they tap into archetypes of public governance. They can be used as springboards for reflection on how the different perspectives are or can be interconnected and thus how different understandings of trust, explicitly or implicitly, come into play and have an impact on one another in modern public organizations. Our main concern in this book is how the relational approach can challenge the institutional and, in particular, the economic paradigm. Next step in this effort is to flesh out the substantial content of relational trust – starting with the trust component. We will show how key trust definitions and properties can be read through the relational lens and help us gain an understanding of relational trust that is properly informed by extant trust scholarship.

A Kaleidoscope of Relational Trust

We return to the structural aspects of trust in the following chapters. Next, we will show how different definitional elements of trust are useful for clarifying and giving substance to the meaning and functioning of relational trust. An important distinction in this regard is, again, between trust as a psychological state and trust as a social reality. Some of the theoretical elements we make use of derive from a psychological understanding of trust. Consequently, we need to translate and reinterpret their functioning using the social and relational lens. To iterate, we want to show that there is much more to relational trust than close and affectionate personal relationships. Following Lewis and Weigert (1985), a conceptual treatment of trust needs to recognize its multifaceted character. Thus, trust "has distinct cognitive, emotional, and behavioral dimensions which are merged into a unitary social experience" (ibid., p. 969). In other words, to approach trust sociologically is not to neglect its psychological, cognitive and emotional underpinnings, but to insist on considering these elements in context and to ascribe primacy to the social constitution of trust. It is to consider trust as something that is embodied in social action, interaction, communication – not just as something that is present (or not present) in people's hearts and minds. Our first theoretical theme is the fundamental one that has to do with uncertainty and risk.

Uncertainty and Risk

Trust is constituted by uncertainty and all that we cannot know about how things will turn out in the near or far future. Trust always involves some kind of risk. It is something that you show or give in spite of uncertainty and possible doubts about future actions and outcomes. These features are well captured in the definition of personal trust provided by Gambetta (1988):

> trusting a person means believing that when offered the chance, he or she is not likely to behave in a way that is damaging to us, and trust

will *typically* be relevant when at least one party is free to disappoint the other, free enough to avoid a risky relationship, *and* constrained enough to consider that relationship an attractive option.

(p. 219)

On the one hand, trust, per definition, involves a willingness to expose yourself to risk. On the other, it is a way to reduce complexity that allows you to act with greater freedom in relation to others (see below). Hence, there is both a risk and an opportunity side to trust. Importantly, distrust and control are not just opposites to trust; they are functional equivalents in the sense that they constitute alternative ways of reducing complexity (Luhmann, 2017). To adopt a relational perspective is not to argue that (social) trust is always superior and preferable to its functional equivalents. It is to argue that trust in some relations and contexts is a more productive way to handle uncertainty and complexity.

Uncertainty and risk exposure is to some extent mitigated by institutionalized rules and norms. It holds true for most organizations that perceptions of latent sanctions associated with breach of trust will have some impact on the level of trust among organizational members: "I can trust you to carry out this task and fulfil the agreement we have made because not doing so can have negative repercussions for you. That is, it can lead to an organizational sanction in the form of a reprimand, a warning or termination of your employment". This argument, of course, presupposes that the system of organizational sanctions is perceived as just and effective – and legitimate to activate in the case of breach of trust (which may not be the case in collegial relations). Either way, relational trust takes us beyond any form of structural determinism that we may associate with institutional trust. It is not reducible to rational calculation or to a preoccupation with the sanctions and deterrence of rules and norms. Relational trust puts emphasis on social actors, their (situated) agency and choices. Institutionalized rules and norms do not eliminate uncertainty. They mediate uncertainty and constitute a backdrop for managerial action and decision-making. They do not free managers from the responsibility of making decisions – or from the responsibility (and possible blame) associated with showing trust.

Suspension of Disbelief, "the Leap"

Uncertainty (and the need to reduce complexity) is thus ubiquitous. Under such conditions, trust serves as a suspension of disbelief. To show trust is to anticipate the future and behave *as if* it is certain – in spite of all contingencies and known and unknown uncertainties.

To show trust is to take a leap of faith and act *as if* you are sure about the other, although you can never really be sure that the other person will act in accordance with the trust shown to him or her. Trust reduces complexity and enables action by making a bet on a positive future outcome and excluding negative possibilities from consideration (Luhmann, 2017;

Möllering, 2006). Trust is unthinkable without considerations of time, and Luhmann makes a highly topical point about trust and its relationship to the past, the present and the future. He writes: "Trust can only be secured and maintained in the present. Neither the uncertain future nor even the past can arouse trust, since what has been does not eliminate the possibility of the future discovery of another past" (Luhmann, 2017, p. 15). This is basically the storyline of the many cases of sexual harassment uncovered in the wake of the #MeToo movement. Discoveries of a different, no longer hidden or suppressed past reality leading to a withdrawal of trust, public shaming, cancellation of careers and, in some cases, prosecution and legal punishment. The more general point is that the creation and maintenance of trust is an ongoing effort in the present that is never secured by events in the past or future expectations. The suspension of disbelief (until further notice, until reasons to moderate or withdraw trust materializes) is reflective of how trust increases the tolerance for ambiguity and makes it possible "to *live and act with greater tolerance in relation to events*" (Luhmann, 2017, p. 17).

Positive Expectations ... and the Non-Expected

Trust is thus about creating and living up to positive expectations. Some definitions of trust emphasize predictability, but it is not all forms of predictable behavior that deserve to be associated with trust. Rude, obnoxious, offensive, chauvinistic or abusive behaviors may be predictable, based on prior experiences with certain people, but it makes little sense to speak of having trust in such behaviors. Trust is primarily a matter of positive expectations regarding professional ability, benevolence and integrity (see below). To this we can add the standard repertoire of positive relational effects such as the empowerment of individuals and individual resources and competencies, improved motivation and job satisfaction, better communication and stronger personal and organizational relations (Gargiulo & Ertug, 2006).

More challenging than the standard version, however, is the relationship of trust to what is not expected and what is not self-evident in modern organizations. An action, Luhmann reminds us, is not considered to be personal – a reflection of a conscious, deliberate choice – if it is merely a matter of following instructions or orders of superiors. Therefore, subordinates, if they want to make themselves deserving of personal trust, "must strive to exhibit the utmost industriousness, conscientiousness and readiness to carry out tasks loyally, beyond what is customary practice" (Luhmann, 2017, p. 45). Pure adaptation and role conformity are not enough. They must step into character as acting individuals with a will of their own and not just – unquestioning, perhaps blindly – follow the beaten path and do what is formally and explicitly expected of them. "To be meaningful, trust must go beyond predictability", writes Mayer, Davis and Schoorman (1995, p. 714), for what is missing in this approach is willingness to take risk and be vulnerable. In the words of Luhmann (2017, p. 46): "Acting according to the norm is usually inconspicuous and weak in expression, and therefore is not a suitable base from which love and trust can be generated." On a similar note, Solomon and Flores argue that for trust to be authentic, the trustor must transcend what is expected and predictable. Thus, they speak of *authentic trust* as "trust that is fully self-aware, cognizant of its own conditions and limitations, open to new and unimagined possibilities, based on choice and responsibility rather than the mechanical operations of predictability, reliance and rigid rule-following" (2001, p. 59).

Trust and Distrust as Functional Equivalents

To adopt a relational understanding, then, is a matter of bending and providing a more fine-grained understanding of the positivity of trust. One way to challenge the optimistic bias is to realize that trust and distrust are not only opposites, but also functional equivalents. Distrust also serves to reduce complexity, but in a more limiting and, you might say, cramped way than trust. Building on trust, you can extend your possibilities for action considerably as you do not shy away from and can even find support in uncertain premises. Furthermore, you can reduce the uncertainty of your actions considerably by showing trust – as it can be difficult for others to disappoint the trust that you have shown them. If you start from distrust, in contrast, you will only run a risk to the extent that all possible outcomes have been taken into consideration and breaches of trust can be punished through proper sanctions (Luhmann, 2017). Moreover, there is a tendency for distrust to be confirmed and amplified in social interactions. You may even say that distrust "has the capacity to be *self-fulfilling*, to generate a reality consistent with itself" (Gambetta, 1988, p. 234). There are two reasons for this: one, that distrust has a predilection for concreteness (compared to trust) that can easily lead to disappointment (= conformation of the soundness of a distrustful predisposition), and, two, that communication of distrust can have a performative effect and create distrust on the part of the other (Luhmann, 2017).

An example of the former can be a control measure based on distrust. If it works according to the intended and measurable purpose, this suggests that control – and thus distrust – works. It does what it is supposed to do. If it does not work as intended and lead to desired results, this would seem to indicate that distrust is justified and that there is a need for stricter control. The example is generic and simplified, but it illustrates a fundamental asymmetry between trust and distrust as strategies for reduction of complexity. Distrust is prone to become a self-confirming and vicious cycle. It is more difficult to venture from a position of distrust to a position of trust than it is to visit distrust when starting from a position of trust. One reason being that distrust has a built-in blindness for trust as a positive possibility. Even when distrust is disappointed, this can serve as an affirmation of its negative starting point. When trust is disappointed, it can turn into something else, which may be distrust or lower or thinner trust. In this sense, trust is a more open and flexible strategy than distrust. This is not to say, however, that trust is always the most sound and rational choice. Distrust can in many situations be well-chosen and justified.

Limited Trust

To iterate, trust is not an unconditional good. Trust is not recommendable in all situations and/or relations. Besides, professional trust is usually not a carte blanche or an absolute mandate. We can instead speak of it as being *domain specific* and thus limited (Mayer et al., 1995) – in the sense that it most often relates to particular abilities, skills or proven strong points of the trustee. As when the trustor has trust in the trustee's ability to handle a particular task or solve a particular problem, while there are other tasks and problems that the trustee is not expected to be able to deal with as competently (or at all). Managers will usually have a sense of what professional, technical and/or social skills of particular employees they can put trust in and rely on.

There are, however, other basic factors of trustworthiness than *ability*. Mayer et al. (1995) also mention *benevolence* and *integrity*. While ability lends itself to domain specificity, due to its focus on specific skills and competencies, benevolence and integrity are not so easily partitioned. For instance, an employee's assessment of the benevolence or integrity of a manager will not usually be dividable into categories of benevolence in regard to specific tasks or integrity in regard to others. It will more likely be reflected in an overall assessment of how trustworthy the manager is based on these criteria: how benevolent the manager appears in regard to the individual employee or the group or part of the organization the employee belongs to, and the personal and moral integrity the manager showcases over time (on managerial self-presentation, see Chapter 6). That being said, benevolence and integrity can be a domain of their own; as when there is doubt about a manager's professional ability even though there is high trust in his or her good intentions and moral fiber.

This leads us to the more radical version of the argument regarding domain specificity. It suggests that trust *and* mistrust can be present in the same social relation. Instead of positing trust and mistrust as opposite ends of a spectrum, they can be regarded as separate scales or dimensions. The starting point being that professional relations are complex, dynamic and multifaceted and that this in turn means that balance and consistency are temporary and fleeting accomplishments. Instead, ambiguity can be the norm and high bandwidth and multiplex and segmented relations become the rule rather than the exception (Lewicki, McAllister & Bies, 1998). Instead of considering trust and distrust as a matter of either/or, this way of thinking gives us four combinations to work with: Low trust/Low distrust, Low trust/High distrust, High trust/Low distrust and High trust/High distrust, the latter combination being by far the most interesting and thought-provoking.

Lewicki et al. (1998) suggest that High trust/High distrust is the most prevalent combination of the four and we have personally witnessed that it resonates with the practical experiences of many public managers. What makes it thought-provoking is the underlying suggestion that professional relationships can simultaneously be imbued with faith and confidence (High trust) and fear and skepticism (High distrust). Hence, Lewicki et al. (1998, p. 443) associate high distrust with "confident negative expectations", that is, "a fear of, a propensity to attribute sinister intentions to, and a desire to buffer oneself from the effects of another's conduct". While the resulting "Trust but verify" mentality makes good sense in interorganizational relationships involving collaboration and negotiation between separate juridical entities, economic transactions and contractual obligations, it is arguably harder to reconcile with the trust ideals of intraorganizational relationships. Relational trust is far removed from fear and skepticism, and it is worth asking whether this conceptualization ultimately gives the upper hand to distrust. What room is left for High trust to make a positive difference if High distrust is always present? Following Van de Walle and Six (2014, p. 162), distrust as confident negative expectations is bound to "colour all aspects of interaction, and influence even the most basic perceptions of the other, resulting in a very biased view of 'reality'". However, a possible explanation for the resonance found among public managers can be that they (as well as public employees) do not always get to choose themselves who to collaborate with, but can be more or less forced into particular relational engagements. This can in turn lead to situations where there is a perceived need on the part of the trustor to show good will (High trust), while prior experiences may indicate that the trustee is difficult to work with and not particularly trustworthy (High distrust). Again, the question is whether such relations deserve to be labelled as trusting or whether the net outcome of combining High trust and High distrust is a low level of trust with limited bandwidth. Either way, this conceptualization provides an intriguing take on the social limitations of trust and the intersections between trust and distrust. The more moderate version of the same argument suggests that trust is, again, domain specific without making inferences about the simultaneous prevalence of distrust, fear, skepticism and wariness.

Accept of Vulnerability

It was Rousseau et al. (1998) who first proposed accept of vulnerability as a cross-cutting theme that can serve to unify different understandings of trust. Before that, however, a number of research contributions going back to Deutsch (1962) and Zand (1972) have put emphasis on vulnerability as a defining feature of trust relations (Hosmer, 1995). Mayer et al. (1995, p. 712, original emphasis) proposed a definition of trust as

> the *willingness of a party to be vulnerable to the actions of another party based on the expectation that the other will perform a particular action important to the trustor, irrespective of the ability to control or monitor that other party.*

Vis-à-vis the notion of "willingness" in the above definition, Rousseau et al. defined trust as "a psychological state comprising the intention to accept vulnerability based upon positive expectations of the intentions or behavior of another" (Rousseau et al., 1998, p. 395). This is a psychological definition taking its point of departure in the mind of the individual trustor. To make it social and relational, we have to add a behavioral and action-oriented dimension. You are not running any risk just because you are, according to your own thought-process and self-narrative, willing to accept vulnerability and in this sense have trust. The intention to accept vulnerability is not a sufficient qualifier. It is only when the intention becomes manifest in a particular action or behavior in relation to others that something is at stake. Mayer et al. (1995) are aware of this difference. They write:

> There is no risk taken in the *willingness* to be vulnerable (i.e., to trust), but risk is inherent in the *behavioral manifestation* of the willingness to be vulnerable. One does not need to risk anything in order to trust; however, one must take a risk in order to engage in trusting action. The fundamental difference between trust and trusting behaviors is between a "willingness" to assume risk and actually "assuming" risk. Trust is the willingness to assume risk; behavioral trust is the *assuming* of risk.
>
> (p. 724)

This quote helps us further clarify how a social and relational understanding of trust differs from a psychological understanding. We strongly emphasize the workings of trust as a behavioral and communicative phenomenon – as opposed to a willingness in people's heads that may potentially lead to certain actions.

Defining accept of vulnerability as a psychological state makes it possible to avoid questions regarding the cultural meaning of being vulnerable and showing vulnerability. However, such questions are unavoidable when you apply a relational lens and insist that trust is about action and talk. Vulnerability is, on the one hand, culturally associable with weakness (see below); on the other, it takes courage and strength for managers to accept vulnerability in relation to an employee or a group of employees – in expectation of positive intentions (on the part of the others) and a positive outcome. Accept of vulnerability is here taken to mean an antiauthoritarian stance where the manager knowingly and willingly exposes himself or herself to being corrected, contradicted or having managerial decisions and actions – past, present or future – challenged. The very opposite of this is a "Yes" culture where it is illegitimate to challenge the authority, decisions and actions of a particular manager or of management, where dissent is frowned upon and where open dialog and exchange of ideas are absent. "Yes" culture, however, is not a sign of strength on the part of managers, but rather indicative of a lack of trust either in their own professional capacities or social skills or in the intentions, willingness and ability of employees to contribute professionally and constructively to an open exchange. This can in turn lead to an enormous loss of information and lack of effective coordination of joint efforts. Willingness to accept vulnerability is ultimately a precondition for managers to meet employees with the kind of openness and benevolence that we normally associate with trust.

Another question has to do with whether or how this kind of acceptance needs to be considered as gendered. Fletcher (2004) and Fletcher and Käufer (2003) argue that the traits associated with relational – post-heroic – models of leadership tend to be seen as feminine (see also Fondas, 1997). Both men and women can display them, "but the traits themselves – such as empathy, community, vulnerability, and skills of inquiry and collaboration – are socially ascribed to women in our culture and generally understood as feminine" (Fletcher & Käufer, 2003, p. 34). Conversely, the attributes associated with heroic leadership (individualism, control, assertiveness, domination etc.) are socially attributed to men and generally seen as masculine (ibid.). As they also point out, conventional wisdom has pathologized an attribute like vulnerability, often characterizing it as a weakness, a psychological deficiency or a sign of personal inadequacy. Hence, vulnerability is culturally associable with weakness. As in: "to be vulnerable helps is to be weak". According to an authoritarian mindset or very traditional notions of managerial power, it would follow that "to accept vulnerability is to accept weakness". Crevani, Lindgren and Packendorff (2007, p. 49) similarly speak of how post-heroic leadership practices "are unconsciously associated with femininity and powerlessness". Certainly, we can find both alpha males and alpha females who would subscribe to such a creed and to what must, from a trust perspective, be considered an outmoded understanding of managerial strength. More important, for present purposes, is the question of whether male and female managers, regardless of their disposition, are subject to different expectations and attributions when it comes to their acceptance of vulnerability. In other words, are female managers more likely to be associated with the willingness and ability to accept vulnerability than male managers? Conversely, are male managers more likely to associate vulnerability with weakness and to seek to avoid appearing vulnerable? And how can such matters be addressed without inadvertently reifying gender differences and perpetuating gender stereotypes? (See also our discussion of post-heroic leadership and gender in Chapter 3.)

Sense and Sensibility

The same types of questions apply to the emotional component of relational trust. To iterate, prior research has tended to give the institutional and economic brands of system trust the cognitive and rational upper hand by strongly emphasizing the affective and identification-based aspects of social trust. Although we find this emotional overdetermination of social trust problematic, we do recognize that there is an emotional aspect to relational trust that we need to account for. Indeed, relational trust is based on a combination of cognitive and emotional elements. If you remove all emotional content, you are left with rational prediction (akin to economic trust), and if you remove all cognitive content, you are entirely in the throes of emotions (and associated risks of irrational behavior, blind or blue-eyed trust; Gargiulo & Ertug, 2006; Lewis & Weigert, 1985). In other words, we do, for better or worse, have to consider trust as a phenomenon that transcends rationality and involves emotional bonds. In the words of Lewis and Weigert (1985):

> The sociological foundation of trust is (...) constructed on an *emotional* base that is complementary to its cognitive base. This affective component of trust consists in an emotional bond among all those who participate in the relationship. Like the affective bonds of friendship and love, trust creates a social situation in which intense emotional investments may be made, and this is why the betrayal of a personal trust arouses a sense of emotional outrage in the betrayed. The betrayal of trust strikes a deadly blow at the foundation of the relationship itself, not merely at the specific content of the betrayal. This emotional component is present in all types of trust, but it is normally most intense in close interpersonal trust.
>
> (p. 971)

We have to take account of how betrayal of trust can be taken "personally" and result in hurt feelings, even in professional relationships. In the words of Solomon and Flores (2001, p. 58): "Trust is not a *feeling*." By this, they mean to say that "there is no feeling of trust as such, and reducing trust to a feeling ignores the interactive and dynamic aspects of trust in favor of a more or less passive 'intuition'" (ibid.). To iterate, a relational understanding of trust (rooted in sociology) does not give explanatory primacy to emotions. Nevertheless, as Solomon and Flores also acknowledge, we need to consider how trust is inextricably involved with emotions and moods.

Moreover, trust is such a fundamental value that it can create a sense of awkwardness or feel like a violation if distrust or lack of trust is shown or communicated directly and in no uncertain terms between two parties; it can be a manager and an employee or a group of employees. Solomon and Flores (2001) speak of *cordial hypocricy* as a way to keep up appearances and maintain a façade of goodwill and congeniality – even if distrust and cynicism are lurking underneath. Of course, a cordial façade has little to do with trust, but it can blind organizations to problems of distrust. Solomon and Flores even suggest that denial, not distrust, can be the greatest enemy of trust. While denial can serve to maintain harmony, minimize frictions and avoid conflicts here and now (in the short term, superficially), its shortcomings are bound to become apparent in the long term. If trust is only a matter of pretense, the lack of authenticity is bound to show.

To experience other's lack of trust can be an unbearable emotional burden to carry for an individual, just as the experience of having distrust toward others is bound to result in a lowered sense of emotional well-being. Conversely, it is bound to give the individual a better sense of well-being to be met with and have trust in others. The realization that emotions matter is not least important when it comes to dealing with situations involving breaches of trust or lack of trust. Problems of distrust can in many (if not most) instances not be dealt with by appeal to only rational capacities and-learning.

Trust as Process

The final point we want to make about trust in this chapter is that it needs to be considered in a process perspective. Process is part and parcel of viewing trust as a relational, experience-based and emergent phenomenon (Möllering, 2013). Trust is not a stable state or condition, but always in movement in social processes, interactions and transactions involving managers and employees situated in organizational contexts. In organizational settings, trust is about much more than the individual and dyadic, interpersonal relations. Trust is embedded, in various ways, in the institutionalized structures, rules and norms of modern public organizations. Even the economizing pull of market thinking embodies its own – albeit negative – view of trust and its own set of recommendations regarding trust. Economic trust in turn has its polar opposite in moral trust. Relational trust is thus accompanied by other approaches that could lead to different starting points for managerial engagement with trust. What sets the relational approach apart, however, is its reflective ability not only to harbor important insights about (and prescriptions regarding) the social workings of trust, but also to incorporate insights from the other approaches and from other concepts and discourses into its view of modern public organizations.

In the next chapter, we pursue the relational line of reasoning further, our main focus being the relationship between trust and power. It would be sociologically naïve to make trust-based leadership into an instrumental or normative matter of paving the way for more trust in modern organizations – without further ado. This chapter has already taken us beyond such simplified notions. We also have to account for the workings of power, that is, the intricate intersections and (im)balances between trust and power and substitutive or complementary relations between trust and control. This is what we turn to in Chapter 3, where we also touch on matters of debureaucratization, post-bureaucracy and post-heroic leadership.

References

Adler, P. S. (2001). Market, hierarchy, and trust: The knowledge economy and the future of capitalism. *Organization Science*, 12(2), 215–234.

Bevan, D. & Corvellec, H. (2007). The impossibility of corporate ethics: For a Lévinasian approach to managerial ethics. *Business Ethics – A European Journal*, 16(3), 208–219.

Blomqvist, K. (1997). The many faces of trust. *Scandinavian Journal of Management*, 13(3), 271–286.

Bouckaert, G. (2012a). Reforming for performance and trust: Some reflections. *The NISPAcee Journal of Public Administration and Policy*,V(1), 9–20.

Bouckaert, G. (2012b). Trust and public administration. *Administration*, 60(1), 91–115.

Casson, M. & Della Giusta, M. (2006).The economics of trust. In R. Bachmann & A. Zaheer (Eds.). *Handbook of trust research* (332–354). Cornwall: Edward Elgar.

Choudhury, E. (2008). Trust in administration: An integrative approach to optimal trust. *Administration & Society*, 40(6), 586–620.

Cohen, M. A. & Dienhart, J. (2013). Moral and amoral conceptions of trust, with an application in organizational ethics. *Journal of Business Ethics*, 112, 1–13.

Coleman, J. S. (1990). *The foundations of social theory*. Cambridge, MA: Harvard University Press.

Crevani, L., Lindgren, M. & Packendorff, J. (2007). Shared leadership: A postheroic perspective on leadership as a collective construction. *International Journal of Leadership Studies*, 3(1), 40–67.

Dasgupta, P. (1988). Trust as a commodity. In D. Gambetta (Ed.). *Trust: Making and breaking cooperative relations* (49–72). Oxford: Blackwell.

Deutsch, M. (1962). Cooperation and trust: Some theoretical notes. In *Nebraska symposium on motivation* (275–320). Lincoln: Nebraska University Press.

Ferraro, F., Pfeffer, J. & Sutton, R. I. (2005). Economics language and assumptions: How theories can become self-fulfilling. *Academy of Management Review*, 30(1), 8–24.

Fletcher, J. K. (2004). The paradox of postheroic leadership: An essay on gender, power, and transformational change. *The Leadership Quarterly*, 15(5), 647–661.

Fletcher, J. K. & Käufer, K. (2003). Shared leadership: Paradox and possibility. Ch. 2 in C. L. Pearce & J. A. Conger (Eds.). *Shared leadership: Reframing the hows and whys of leadership* (21–47).Thousand Oaks, CA: Sage.

Fondas, N. (1997). Feminization unveiled: Management qualities in contemporary writing. *Academy of Management Review*, 22(1), 257–282.

Fox, A. (1974). *Beyond contract: Work, power and trust relations*. London: Faber & Faber.

Gambetta, D. (1988). Can we trust trust? In D. Gambetta (Ed.) (1988). *Trust: Making and breaking cooperative relations* (213–237). Oxford: Blackwell.

Gargiulo, M. & Ertug, G. (2006).The dark side of trust. In R. Bachmann & A. Zaheer (Eds.). *Handbook of trust research* (165–186). Cornwall: Edward Elgar.

Grey, C. & Garsten, C. (2001). Trust, control and post-bureaucracy. *Organization Studies*, 22(2), 229–250.

Hosmer, L. T. (1995).Trust:The connecting link between organizational theory and philosophical ethics. *Academy of Management Review*, 20(2), 379–403.

Jagd, S. (2009). Tillidsbaseret ledelse – en ny udfordring for ledere. *Ledelse & Erhvervsøkonomi*, 3, 7–21.

Lagerspetz, O. (1998). *Trust: The tacit demand*. Dordrecht: Springer Science+Business Media.

Lane, J.-E. (2000). *New public management*. London: Routledge.

Lewicki, R. J. & Bunker, B. B. (1996). Developing and maintaining trust in work relationships. In R. M. Kramer & T. R. Tyler (Eds.). *Trust in organizations: Frontiers of theory and research* (114–139).Thousand Oaks: Sage.

Lewicki, R. J., McAllister, D. J. & Bies, R. J. (1998).Trust and distrust: New relationships and realities. *Academy of Management Review*, 23(3), 438–458.

Lewis, J. D. & Weigert, A. (1985).Trust as a social reality. *Social Forces*, 63(4), 967–985.

Luhmann, N. (1979). *Trust and power*. New York: Wiley.

Luhmann, N. (2017). *Trust and power*. St. Ives: Polity Press.

Løgstrup, K. E. (1997). *The ethical demand*. Indiana: University of Notre Dame Press.

Mayer, R. C., Davis, J. H. & Schoorman, F. D. (1995). An integrative model of organizational trust. *Academy of Management Review*, 20(3), 709–734.

McAllister, D. J. (1995). Affect- and cognition-based trust as foundations for interpersonal cooperation in organizations. *Academy of Management Journal*, 38, 24–59.

Möllering, G. (2006). *Trust: Reason, routine, reflexivity*. Bingley: Emerald.

Möllering, G. (2013). Process views of trusting and crises. In R. Bachmann & A. Zaheer (Eds.). *Handbook of advances in trust research* (285–305). Padstow: Edward Elgar.

Monteiro, P. & Adler, P. S. (2022). Bureaucracy for the 21st century: Clarifying and expanding our view of bureaucratic organization. *Academy of Management Annals*. Preprint version. https://doi.org/10.5465/annals.2019.0059

Oomsels, P. & Bouckaert, G. (2014). Studying interorganizational trust in public administration: A conceptual and analytical framework for "administrational trust". *Public Performance & Management Review*, 37, 577–604.

Pearce, J. L. (2008). Bureaucracy and trust: A review of recent volumes in the Russell Sage Foundation Series on Trust. *International Public Management Journal*, 11(4), 481–485.

Pollitt, C. & Bouckaert, G. (2011). *Public management reform: A comparative analysis – New public management, governance, and the neo–Weberian State*, 3rd edition. Oxford: Oxford University Press.

Rousseau, D. M., Sitkin, S. B., Burt, R. S. & Camerer, C. (1998). Not so different after all: A cross-discipline view of trust. *Academy of Management Review*, 23(3), 393–404.

Shapiro, S. P. (1987). The social control of impersonal trust. *American Journal of Sociology*, 93, 623–658.

Shapiro, D., Sheppard, B. H. & Cheraskin, L. (1992). Business on a handshake. *Negotiation Journal*, 8, 365–377.

Sheppard, B. H. & Sherman, D. M. (1998). The grammars of trust: A model and general implications. *The Academy of Management Review*, 23(3), 422–437.

Six, F. & Sorge. (2008). Creating a high-trust organization: An exploration into organizational policies that stimulate interpersonal trust building. *Journal of Management Studies*, 45(5), 857–884.

Solomon, R. C. & Flores, F. (2001). *Building trust – in business, politics, relationships and life*. New York, NY: Oxford University Press.

Sztompka, P. (2019). Trust in the moral space. In M. Sasaki (Ed.). *Trust in comtemporary society* (31–40). Boston: Brill.

Tyler, T. R. (2003). Trust within organisations. *Personnel Review*, 32(5), 556–568.

Uslaner, E. M. (2002). *The moral foundations of trust*. New York: Cambridge University Press.

Van de Walle, S. (2011). New public management: Restoring the public trust through creating distrust? In T. Christensen & P. Lægreid (Eds.). *Ashgate research companion to new public management* (309–320). Aldershot: Ashgate.

Van de Walle, S. (2017). Trust in public administration and public services. In European Commission, Directorate-General for Research and Innovation. *Trust at risk: implications for EU policies and institutions* (118–128). Brussels: Publications Office.

Van de Walle, S. & Six, F. (2014). Trust and distrust as distinct concepts: Why studying distrust in institutions is important. *Journal of Comparative Policy Analysis: Research and Practice*, 16(2), 158–174.

Williamson, O. E. (1993). Calculativeness, trust, and economic organization. *The Journal of Law & Economics*, 36(1), 453–486.

Zand, D. E. (1972). Trust and managerial problem solving. *Administrative Science Quarterly*, 17(2), 229–239.

Zucker, L. G. (1986). Production of trust: Institutional sources of economic structure, 1849–1920. *Research in Organizational Behavior*, 8, 53–111.

3 Trust and Power

Our treatment and conceptualization of the trust paradigms and the workings of relational trust leads us to the question of how trust is to be conceived in relation to power. As previously mentioned, there is a dearth of scholarly reflection on this relationship. There is, albeit with some notable exceptions, a tendency to see trust and power as opposite and mutually exclusive orientations regarding management and governance (Kroeger, 2019). And there is a tendency for research, especially research on organization and management, to focus on trust's positive qualities to the detriment of the messy social reality in which it has to function. The starting point of this chapter is that we always have to account for the workings of trust *and* power. It is not (and never) an either/or and it is important to maintain a reflexive awareness of this. Speaking of trust in relation to leadership, management and governance inextricably evokes notions of power: in organizational and professional settings, trust is not (or rarely) an end in itself, but a means to an end. It is part of efforts to lead, manage, motivate and even, some will say, control people. Sydow (1998, p. 31) thus speaks of how "in a world of increasing uncertainty and complexity, flat hierarchies, more participatory management styles and increasing professionalism, trust is thought to be a more appropriate mechanism for controlling organizational life". Furthermore, in modern public organizations, the workings of trust are explicitly entangled with different forms of governance and managerial power and control. Our treatment of the trust paradigms and the tug-of-war between different models of public governance made this quite apparent, although we did not explicitly address the matter of power.

Turning to this matter, we continue to pursue a relational understanding. That is to say, *with a relational view of trust comes a relational view of power.* This has a number of implications that will become apparent throughout the chapter. Most importantly, perhaps, a relational frame of understanding makes it possible to argue that *trust and power are two sides of the same coin*, but this in turn calls for a clarification of what relational power means in theory and in practice. We use the work of Foucault on power as a positive and productive force to support this argument. Grey and Garsten (2001, p. 232) have argued that trust can be viewed as a specific form of power, and that while "some exercises of power cannot be understood in terms of trust, (…)

DOI: 10.4324/9780429431104-3

no instances of trust can be understood as separate from power". We concur with this important point, and our particular take on it is that a relational theory of trust calls for a relational theory of power.

To iterate, not all – authoritative, repressive – uses of power are conducive to trust or deserving of the moniker trust. We need to clarify why and how uses of power can be considered as trust-based or reflective of trust. We proceed with a depiction of how relational trust is linked to a productive understanding of power. This leads us into reflections on the relationship between trust and control, the so-called trust-control nexus. Next, we look at how questions of control and autonomy are reflected in various forms of debureaucratization – a concept closely associated with the emergence of the *post-bureaucratic organization*. The literature on post-bureaucratic organization allows for critical reflection not only on the relationship between trust and power, but also more fundamentally on the organizational implications of a turn toward greater reliance on trust. With this focus on post-bureaucracy, the reflexive, theory-driven and occasionally normative route taken in this book intersects with *critical management studies*, which tend to harbor a skeptical view of "Theory" as a modernist and reifying endeavor. Critical management studies are prone to consider organizational imperatives regarding trust as little more than a surface phenomenon masking underlying instrumental imperatives and structures of domination (just as New Public Governance [NPG] can be construed as a thin veneer masking the continued dominance of a New Public Management [NPM] mindset). We find that critical management studies pose some relevant challenges to trust-based leadership that need to be addressed. After weaving these critical insights into our theoretical narrative, we continue to pursue developments in self-management, post-heroic, distributed and shared leadership and how they can shed light on relationships between trust and power.

Finally, after addressing the relationship between trust and values, we turn to questions of motivation and motivation crowding. While most of the chapter draws on a qualitative and relational sociological research tradition, much of what has been written about management and motivation in the public sector is built on economic theory and quantitative studies. On the one hand, this literature illustrates some of the difficulties involved in approaching issues of trust in a nuanced and granular manner while building on assumptions taken from economic theory. On the other, concepts such as "public service motivation" (PSM), "knights and knaves" and "motivation crowding" are not just essential for understanding management challenges in the public sector, they are also helpful as means to refine our understanding of how trust can motivate public sector employees and, more generally, how perceptions of trustworthiness become a factor in how management and governance are undertaken.

Trust and Power in a Relational Perspective

Speaking of trust and power together, or of trust as a form of power or mode of governance, our emphasis is on power as something that is (or has the potential to be) positive, productive and non-coercive – as opposed to negative, repressive and authoritarian. In recent years, this kind of power has been codified under headings such as "soft" power and nudging and comes to the fore in post-bureaucratic ideals of management. For an underlying theory or analytics of relational power that can mirror and support our relational view of trust, we turn to the work of Michel Foucault on power and governance (Foucault, 1977, 1978; Faubion, 1994).

As a starting point, Foucault considers power to be omnipresent in social relations. Power is relational, dispersed and operating from multiple centers. Hierarchy and notions of preordained sovereign authority are thus rejected. Instead, we get a view of power that operates closer to the ground and closer to micro-social relations and practices. Power is not something that can be possessed by a ruling body or which rests in formalized structures. Power is performative and manifests itself in action: it is something you *do*, not something you *have*, and it can take the form of counter-power and resistance. Foucault describes it as: "A set of actions upon other actions" (Foucault, 1982, p. 341). The point being that power is different from force or violence. It can only be exercised over individuals or collective actors that have some leeway and freedom to act and make choices. Hence, Foucault presupposes that there is a thinking and acting subject at the other end of the power relation. Although some individuals (managers are obvious examples) do have formal power over others, "such power is not absolute because actors have choices in an imperfect system" (Ettlinger, 2011, p. 549). This is also reflected in his definition of government as a conduct of conduct: a form of conduct that relates to how others conduct themselves (Foucault, 1978, 2009), and which consists not in determining how others should act but in structuring the possible fields of action of others (Foucault, 1982). According to Foucault, power cannot be reduced to a repressive force that operates in the negative form of commands or prohibiting rules; it can be a positive, productive, liberating force that can enable action and empower individuals (Foucault, 1980). Importantly, the same point applies to our treatment of relational power that applied to relational trust: it is a matter of situated agency and must be considered in the context of organizational constraints and enablers. In other words, relational power does not capture all that power is in organizations. It serves to complement repressive understandings focusing on the properties of force and coercion (cf. Lukes, 1974).

In a productive understanding of power, the freedom of organizational members is not a problem to be minimized, but a resource for the exercise of power. It is not about having or wielding power *over* others, but about the ability of managers to become powerful *through* the accomplishments of others. Productive power is thus augmented by other people's trust. The difference that the productive understanding makes can be illustrated by comparison with its direct opposite. According to Robert A. Dahl's classical definition, "A has power over B to the extent that he can get B to do something that B would not otherwise do" (Dahl, 1957, pp. 202–203). This is *the* conceptual archetype of negative and coercive power and a definition that resonates with the institutional and the economic trust paradigm. System trust is thus predicated on repressive power as it assumes that institutionalized rules and norms and market arrangements respectively provide effective means of governing action and serve as deterrents against wrongdoing.

Although repressive power is inextricably linked to organizational structures and processes involving hierarchy and/or market, it does not provide an adequate description of how power works in organizational relationships. Managers are expected to be able to use the formal authority with which their jobs are invested to cut through and make decisions regarding employees' priorities and use of time, their work tasks and, ultimately, their employment, but it is not necessarily these types of controlling power that are most significant with regard to the organization of work and the creation of value. One of the limitations of a definition such as Dahl's is that it associates power exclusively with the ability to decide over others and control and limit what others should do. Consequently, trust and power appear to be substitutes in the sense that showing trust becomes a matter of relinquishing power.

In other words, it is assumed that the relationship between trust and power is akin to a *zero-sum game*: more of one leads to less of the other and vice versa. By contrast, a productive understanding of power allows for the relationship to be considered a *positive-sum* game in which trust serves to support or enhance power. Indeed, trust and power are considered as mutually supportive features of management and leadership. Managers who appear trustworthy, who show trust and are able to build on trust are stronger and more powerful leaders – is the underlying normative message. Instead of considering trust in terms of a loss (of control), it is about understanding trust as an investment in social relations that can make a positive difference both in the short and the long run (see Chapter 4 on social capital). As reflected in notions of post-heroic leadership (see below), management is not only (or primarily) about building and consolidating one's own power base; it is also about empowering others to make the most of their professional and social skills and development potential. In other words, it is about increasing the collective capacity for action and performance.

This in turn means that lack of trust or outright distrust is not seen as a more or less inevitable by-product of the exercise of managerial power, but more as a problem and a potential barrier to effective management and organizational performance. Managers who fail to inspire trust and who – consciously or unconsciously, deliberately or otherwise – communicate mistrust toward others will not reap the benefits of trust as a form of productive power. This does not mean, however, that organizations will necessarily malfunction in the absence of trust. Empirical evidence suggests otherwise. Public, private and voluntary organizations can all function in the short and longer term without any great trust in top management or particular managers. Arguably, they would be short-lived if it was otherwise. The message is that organizations tend to perform better when there is a higher degree of trust, and that this is not only about motivation and well-being, but also about the effective use of professional skills and value creation.

If we argue that trust is something that managers can work with, consciously and purposefully, we must accept that it can be considered a form of power. That is, not only are the workings of trust inextricably linked to mechanisms of power, it is also actually a way to exercise power. You show trust not only or primarily because of a deep-seated disposition, but also in order to lead, motivate and move people. This does not exclude intuitive or spontaneous acts from consideration, but the general point remains: managerial trust is always infused with power, goal directedness and accomplishment. Managerial trust is, as a rule, not an end in itself and not about altruism. This is not meant to suggest a cynical or manipulative approach to trust and management. It is a fundamental premise regarding management that aligns with the assumptions of relational trust (while it may be at odds with moral trust). Indeed, we are not the first to suggest that trust can be considered a form of managerial power or social control that aims to develop or stimulate employees' ability to self-manage or practice self-control (Sprenger, 2004; Jagd, 2009). To iterate, when we say that trust is a form of power, we are referring to a positive and productive understanding of power, not power in general. Relational trust and relational power go hand in hand, and it is with this starting point that we can say that trust and power are two sides of the same coin.

With these reflections regarding trust and power, we are still operating on a high level of generality and painting with broad strokes. Focusing on the relationship between trust and control allows us to move closer in on the concrete challenges that are involved in creating a productive balance between trust and power in modern public organizations.

Trust and Control – Substitutes or Complements?

The relationship between trust and control is a central theme in the trust literature, although there is a tendency for research to focus on either trust or control. Following Möllering (2005, p. 284), our starting point is "that trust and control each assume the existence of the other, refer to each other and create each other, but remain irreducible to each other". Two basic understandings of the relationship proliferate. According to one, trust and control are substitutes and mutually excluding. According to the other, trust and control are complementary and mutually constitutive. In keeping with the above discussion, we find the latter mode of understanding to be the most productive. That is, we find that it has more to offer with regard to understanding and challenging management thinking and development processes in the public sector (see also Edelenbos & Eshuis, 2012). This is not to say, however, that we need to choose between the two perspectives. They both embody important insights, and we will draw on both in the remainder of the chapter. For instance, as we shall see, the notion of a substitutive relationship between trust and control plays an important part in the theoretical framing of PSM and motivation crowding.

Using Luhmann's terminology, trust and control can be considered as functionally equivalent. They both serve to reduce complexity in social relations and exchanges, but they do so in different ways. Trust reduces complexity by focusing on positive outcomes and excluding negative possibilities from view – vis-à-vis the leap of faith Luhmann, 2017). Trust is, again, "a bet on the future contingent actions of others" (Sztompka, 1999, p. 64). Control works by regulating and reducing the number of possible outcomes (Edelenbos & Eshuis, 2012). While trust implies acceptance of uncertainty, control reflects efforts to minimize it (Vallentin & Thygesen, 2017). The substitution view suggests that formal control mechanisms (including codification of rules and norms and surveillance and monitoring of people's behavior and performance) can undermine trust, while in other situations the prevalence of trust can remove or minimize the need for control (Bijlsma-Frankema & Costa, 2005; Khodyakov, 2007). This aligns with one of the preferred narratives in the literature on trust-based leadership: that control is an evil (or certainly inefficient), and that trust is (almost always) preferable. However, if we apply a complementary lens, the picture that emerges is less black and white and more granular. Here, the argument is that elements of trust as well as control enable individuals and groups to work efficiently and that both are essential for the proper functioning of organizations (Bachmann, 2001; Costa & Bijlsma-Frankema, 2007). Not only informal – social – forms of control can engender trust (Bradach & Eccles, 1989). Even formal control mechanisms can serve this function by providing people with objective rules and clear indicators and goals, allowing them to assess each other's abilities, trustworthiness and performance on an ongoing basis (Bijlsma-Frankema & Costa, 2005; Das & Teng, 1998; Long & Sitkin, 2006; Weibel, 2007). In this way, trust and control can enter into a symbiotic relationship and be mutually reinforcing (Edelenbos & Eshuis, 2012).

Turning to practice and the empirical reality in public organizations, both perspectives offer important insights. There are plenty of examples of control obliterating trust, and trust can ideally reduce the need for control in the public sector. In this way, the substitution view can help diagnose widespread trust problems and point toward an ideal solution. However, the complementary view offers a more refined view of the intricate relations and interactions between trust and control encountered in public organizations. As mentioned in Chapter 1, the Danish trust reform does not imply that control is replaced by trust, plain and simple. It is rather a matter of the balance between trust and control being renegotiated and reconfigured in different ways. Keeping in mind the need to understand trust-building as process, trust reform does not constitute a process of radical upheaval in which trust supplants control. It reflects efforts to alter the balance between the two and allow greater room for trust to flourish and make a difference – without sidelining the need for governance and managerial oversight and control. To understand what is happening in this process, we need to be aware of the control side and of the interplay between trust and control – and how managers and employees experience the changes that are taking place. At any rate, focusing exclusively on either trust or control is misleading considering the complex working conditions of public sector organizations and the manifold demands and expectations their management has to cope with (Edelenbos & Eshuis, 2012; Möllering, 2005; Vallentin & Thygesen, 2017).

Control is the problem, trust is the solution. While the substitution view supports this popular (but ultimately reductionist) understanding, the complementary view recognizes that control is not just coercive, but can also be productive – or at least does not have to be unproductive. Discussions of (lack of) trust in the public sector have primarily focused on negative aspects of control, as when bureaucratic red tape seems to become an end in itself or a self-reinforcing mechanism that has a demotivating effect on employees and fails to create value for citizens. However, as per the institutional trust paradigm, control can underpin trust by providing clearly defined rules, goals and measures in relation to management and manager-employee relations. Not all organizational matters are conducive to regulation via social trust. For example, we are better off having wages and basic conditions of employment be based on rules and rights (and associated control mechanisms) rather than (social) trust in managers. Rules can serve a purpose; they speed up processes in situations and in relation to work tasks characterized by routine and low complexity, and documentation is not an evil *per se*. After all, how can trust be generated and maintained in the long run without any measures of whether it is justified? To iterate, it is hard to imagine that a public sector unable to document its accomplishments would be considered properly accountable and worthy of public trust.

Control cuts both ways, and it can be a productive exercise for managers and employees to try and identify which forms of control support and which undermine trust in their organization and in relation to their professional area of expertise. The purpose of the exercise being to identify controls that have a demotivating effect and do not create value for citizens (see Chapter 5). This is not to say, however, that such controls are easily reduced or abolished. Thus, many control mechanisms are embedded in legislation and regulations, which – whether they work as intended or not – are meant to guarantee the rights of citizens. That being said, the trust agenda points to potentials for reducing control and allowing for more productive interactions between trust and control.

An important notion in this regard is *meaning* (which we return to later in the chapter when we address questions of motivation more in-depth). It is important that control is meaningful, that it makes sense in a productive way (see Fuglsang & Jagd, 2013, on trust and sensemaking), and that managers and employees experience that the types of control their work is subjected to either, ideally, enable them to do their jobs better and more effectively, or, more realistically, does not seem meaningless and demotivating. If control is experienced as meaningless, it will act as a disincentive. This does not reduce the managerial challenge to one of effective *sensegiving*, communicating and influencing people's experiences regarding extant control systems (cf. Gioia & Chittipeddi, 1991). The trust agenda also points to a need for actually changing how control systems work. However, keeping in mind that control systems and documentation requirements are here to stay in one form or another, the sensemaking task is bound to remain an important one. That is, it will remain an ongoing challenge for public managers to either make control systems seem meaningful, or at least avoid that they have a negative and demotivating effect and undermine trust.

Debureaucratization – Hierarchy and Market

The control issue is a central feature in trust-based efforts to debureaucratize the public sector. Debureaucratization serves as a sort of placeholder for the trust agenda. Depending on context, it can be a more efficient heading for reform efforts. Even those who find trust to be a difficult concept to work with can be enthusiastic about prospects of creating a less bureaucratic public sector. Ultimately, the two agendas are overlapping.

In an early article on debureaucratization, Eisenstadt (1959) argued that literature on bureaucracy tends to shift between two points of view. One defines bureaucracy as a tool or mechanism supporting the successful and efficient implementation of certain goals. Bureaucracy is thus seen as an epitome of rationality and as an embodiment of efficient implementation and provision of services. The other views bureaucracy as an instrument of power and as a corruptible and not necessarily efficient way to exercise control over people and different spheres of life. This perspective is preoccupied with the continued expansion of such power, either in the interest of bureaucracy itself or in the interests of particular elite social actors with vested interests, be it politicians or public administrators. Whereas our treatment of bureaucracy in Chapter 2, under the heading of Institutional Trust, mainly subscribes to the former understanding of bureaucracy, the modern debureaucratization agenda reflects the latter more critical understanding. It focuses on the sociopolitical reality of modern public organization and looks for alternatives or correctives to bureaucratic governance.

To begin with, debureaucratization refers to two interrelated reform efforts or areas of contention. One is preoccupied with hierarchy, the other with market. The former seeks to roll back the "tyranny of rules" associated with the workings of the classical or Neo-Weberian bureaucracy, whereas the latter is concerned with effects of marketization and the market-based forms of bureaucratization that comes with NPM. To be clear, what we engage in here is not a general and constitutive critique of the functioning of bureaucracy, but rather more targeted critiques aiming to reform and improve particular aspects of its functioning. We thus embrace the sociological ambivalence of bureaucracy (Adler, 2012).

Targeted reduction of the rule-based functioning of bureaucracy is, according to the trust agenda, a matter of liberating public sector employees from red tape and documentation requirements that prevent them from utilizing their resources and capabilities in the most productive, meaningful and valuable way – in the best interest of citizens. Critics tend to consider bureaucracy as an organizational form that "is incompatible with complex, dynamic, and individualistic societies" and needs to be replaced by "enterprise, market or network organization, and nonlegal, 'soft' means of governance" (Olsen, 2008, p. 14). The problem, according to this take on debureaucratization, is that the public sector is too hierarchical, too rule-bound and too inflexible, and that this is in turn has harmful effects on economic efficiency and individual freedoms (ibid.).

To use a popular formulation, there is a tendency in the public sector for new rules to be shoveled on, while old ones are removed with tweezers (Produktivitetskommissionen, 2014) – despite occasional declarations of positive political intent regarding rule reduction and more freedom and flexibility for public sector employees. Indeed, it is usually much easier to add layers of regulation than to reduce regulation. One reason for this being that each rule or set of rules are often part of a larger rule complex or political settlement. Public sector organizations are politically governed, and the role and responsibility of politicians in creating and maintaining what some see as a tyranny of rules is undeniable. When critical cases of wrongdoing in the public sector are exposed publicly, the knee-jerk political reaction is often to call for stricter rules and regulation, more control and more documentation, in order to ensure – and send a clear signal – that something similar will not be allowed to happen again. What may turn out to be local problems calling for local action and local solutions instead become generalized, resulting in more rules and constraints for everyone else working in the same field. This can in turn lead to a negative and self-reinforcing spiral of distrust and demotivation.

For users of public services and the citizenry in general, there is both an upside and a downside to reliance upon rules, regulations and related control systems. The upside is that rules come with rights and duties and confer security and predictability. The downside is that rules can be manifest in sluggish case processing following the letter of the law, resulting in impersonal and inflexible treatment without consideration of individual circumstances and needs. Rules are ambivalent and point to a possible schism in trust-based management and governance. With trust-based management, it is usually (if only implicitly) assumed that what is good for public sector employees is good for public service users, but this causality is by no means certain. Trust may be good for individual employees and their sense of self-determination, recognition and belonging, but the benefits to end user are less tangible. With trust comes promises of more personal presence, more personalized treatment, and recognition of the citizen as an individual with particular needs and resources. However, greater reliance on the individual employee's sound judgment also makes the service delivery less predictable and assured. This may in turn not be conducive to T1 trust. There is currently limited evidence showing that more trust and less control (internally) lead to better performance and better service for end users (externally). This is not to say that it does not, but the relationship may be hard to measure, and prior research on T3 trust has mostly focused on internal conditions regarding management and governance. We return to the issue of performance and measurement in Chapters 4 and 5.

Turning to the market-based bureaucratization of the public sector, it is often seen to reflect distrust or lack of trust toward public sector employees. Targeting NPM, debureaucratization is a matter of rolling back elements of economic governance or moderating the management tools that this model makes use of. Of course, NPM can, in itself, be considered a form of debureaucratization as it advocates displacement of traditional bureaucratic norms with market norms (see below), leading some commentators to argue for the need to protect government bureaucracy against the influx of neoliberal reforms – because they can fuel an anti-bureaucratic spirit and undermine values that are critical to the functioning of modern state bureaucracies (Monteiro & Adler, 2022; Siltala, 2013). However, our focus is the post-NPM reform narrative as we take aim at the (paradoxical, perverse) rebureaucratizing effects of NPM and how they can be addressed and remedied.

Efforts to roll back elements of economic governance most often reflect disappointment with the outcomes of NPM. At a general level, this disappointment can be explained in terms of the functioning and malfunctioning of public quasi-markets. NPM endeavors to create market (or market-like) relationships in the public sector and is based on a critique of public sector organization as being unruly and ineffective. It aims to transform public institutions into more effective and user-oriented public organizations through the use of market models, economic governance and management tools emulating the private sector. Uses of contract management, outsourcing, consumer choice and user payment are examples of this (Lund et al., 2008). NPM involves disaggregation, as the work flow is decomposed into atomistic, measurable and benchmarkable units (activities, deliverables, key performance indicators) that are supposed to provide a more effective and transparent basis for managing and developing the public sector. The structural equivalent to this is the decomposition of public organization into autonomous business units that operate as independent profit centers pursuing independent strategies (Monteiro & Adler, 2022). Thus, NPM is founded on the basic (neoliberal) idea that the market is a more effective form of social regulation and development than the bureaucracy (Kamp et al., 2013).

As mentioned in Chapter 1, the empirical reality of NPM over the last couple of decades has often failed to support this idea. NPM is based on a range of supposedly universal and rational principles of economic governance that are meant to facilitate better control over the public economy (Melander, 2008). And yet, in countries like the United Kingdom, Denmark and Sweden, it has been difficult to demonstrate clear efficiency gains or lower costs when applying the tools of NPM (Hartman, 2011; Hood & Dixon, 2015; Kamp et al., 2013). In Denmark, at local government level (municipalities), increased competition in service areas such as home care has in many instances led to higher costs, which is in part due to increased costs of visitation, follow-up and control.

The fundamental problem is that public sector quasi-markets, like other markets, are incapable of effective self-regulation. To make such market mechanisms function in practice, external regulation is required. In order to create a market that, in principle, ensures an equal competitive playing field for all service providers (both public and private), it is necessary to formalize service offerings. This requires careful specification of services – precisely what they consist in, how users qualify for them and how they are to be delivered. Market orientation and exposure to competition thus require an additional layer of economic machine bureaucracy that specifies services, controls delivery and complements the professional bureaucracy. Consequently, market governance often creates more, not less, bureaucracy as it imposes regulation and formal requirements: quality standards, documentation and accreditation requirements and so on (Kamp et al., 2013). This points to what we may term the *paradox of marketization* as advocated by NPM: that efforts meant to free public organizations from the shackles of bureaucracy can turn out to have the opposite (perverse) effect.

The marketization embodied by NPM is, in itself, supposed to represent a form of debureaucratization under the mantra: "more market, less hierarchy". However, in spite of the underlying penchant for privatization, NPM often has the opposite effect of what is intended: it leads to *rebureaucratization* rather than debureaucratization in the sense that it saddles public organizations with more bureaucratic requirements. Speaking of debureaucratization in terms of trust, then, is not just a matter of pointing to limitations of the economic trust paradigm; it is also a matter of addressing the rebureaucratization effects of economic governance.

Post-Bureaucracy and Critical Management Studies

However, debureaucratization is not only a functional matter pertaining to rule reduction and rolling back of NPM. It also, in a more political and symbolic sense, signifies new management discourses and new demands and expectations regarding public-sector managers and employees. One label for this is *post-bureaucratic forms of organization and organizing*. Post-bureaucratic tendencies are found both in the public and the private sector. Post-bureaucratic organization is brought to bear in efforts to reduce formal layers of hierarchy, to focus on flexibility rather than rule-following, and to put consensus, shared values and sense of mission before traditional authority (Grey & Garsten, 2001; Heckscher, 1994). This discourse centers on prospects of liberation and self-determination of organizational members accompanied by a shared sense of purpose – to the supposed benefit of organizational performance and capacity to change.

Post-bureaucratic developments promise "to sweep away the inefficiencies and dysfunctions of creaking bureaucracies" (Hodgson, 2004, p. 83). But what to make of the proposed emancipation of organizational members? This is where critical management studies enter the picture, posing the general theme of *bureaucracy as domination* (Monteiro & Adler, 2022). The critical discourse on post-bureaucracy builds on Marxist thinking as developed in labor process theory (Braverman, 1974; Maravelias, 2003). It suggests that post-bureaucratic organization, under its liberal façade, involves sophisticated forms of managerial domination. The notion of post-bureaucracy as an emancipatory regime is thus a way of masking underlying imperatives regarding instrumental efficiency and control (Barley & Kunda, 1992). Organizational culture, self-organizing teamwork and empowerment programs play important roles in subtle systems of domination where professional freedom and trust are only surface phenomena. Furthermore, post-bureaucracy is seen to differ from conventional notions of bureaucracy in its involvement of the whole individual in organizational practices (Maravelias, 2003) and in its use of indirect and internalized (cultural, ideological) forms of control (Hodgson, 2004). Critical management studies have shown how organizational culture, including the values, norms and beliefs of organizational members, have been absorbed into the instrumental logic of managerialism (Fleming & Spicer, 2003). As a result, management has increasingly become a matter of "managing the 'insides' – the hopes, fears and aspirations – of workers rather than their behaviors directly" (Deetz, 1995, p. 87). Culture building and similar technologies are thus considered as systems of management control that aim to colonize the identities of workers in order to make them more tractable and productive (Fleming & Spicer, 2003). One way to frame this is to speak of "engineered selves" (Kunda, 1992).

According to this kind of narrative, post-bureaucratic organization makes it the responsibility of each individual to take part in engineering and reengineering identities and roles as they relate to work tasks, work boundaries and measures of (self-)evaluation. Organizational members are thus construed as individuals who willingly and actively take part in their own self-government (Maravelias, 2003). In the words of Maravelias (2003, p. 562), post-bureaucracy is more totalitarian than bureaucracy "because it lacks clear boundaries, it is continually present, and seeks to subordinate aspects of the personalities and social networks of individuals to the requirements of instrumental role-playing". He also suggests that what drives individuals to work harder and smarter in post-bureaucratic organizing is often not pressure to subordinate themselves to a clearly defined control regime, but rather the lack of any clearly defined system to subordinate oneself to.

As mentioned previously (Chapter 1), we assume a complex and layered reality in modern public organizations. That is, post-bureaucratic developments are taking place alongside other organizational developments and its favored modes of power and control need to be considered alongside existing bureaucratic frameworks (Fournier, 1999; Hodgson, 2004). While critical management studies aim to debunk post-bureaucratic ideals of freedom and emancipation and show that there is control and domination beneath, we maintain a belief in the power of trust to make a positive difference (and be something other than empty, debunkable rhetoric). However, the critical discourse on post-bureaucratic organization does pose some relevant challenges to the more normative course we steer in this book. It forces us to address the risk of trust becoming a turbo charger for some of the more problematic tendencies inherent to post-bureaucratic organizing. We do not have to assume an ulterior motive regarding neo-bureaucratic control from above (top-down; Hodgson, 2004) to realize that there can be a downside to some of the defining features of relational trust. That is, its embrace of self-determination, open-endedness, uncertainty and risk. As Maravelias (2003) points out, post-bureaucratic work can lead to self-actualization or self-exhaustion. It is supposed to involve a higher level of trust, to be more engaging and satisfying, but also more demanding. It does not suffice to carry out your work tasks with duty and care. Something more existential is at stake. Post-bureaucratic work demands "inner fire" and self-management – and exerts internal pressure on individuals to perform that often surpasses explicit external demands or pressures. Post-bureaucratic organization is thus reflective of modern workplace issues regarding boundarylessness, work-life balance, stress and burnout.

In sum, critical management studies provide us with an important problematization of organizational trust as a post-bureaucratic phenomenon. Critical management studies prescribe a certain wariness regarding emancipatory rhetoric and its organizational implications and outcomes. Although we do acknowledge this problem, our approach differs in three important respects. One, our proposed complementary view of trust and power (and trust and control) is one way to argue for a balanced view of the two – instead of allowing the real politics of power to crowd out or marginalize the importance of social trust. Second, the complementary view of trust and power also leads us to tone down popular notions of trust-based leadership as reflective of liberation or emancipation. What we get instead is a more granular understanding of the intricate relations and balances between trust and power and how they can be negotiated and renegotiated. Third, this boils down to a more open-ended approach to matters of trust and power. Instead of a more or less foregone conclusion and skepticism regarding underlying structures of power and domination, we maintain an openness toward the positive potential of trust.

Keeping in mind our Foucauldian take on power, there are fundamental ontological, epistemological and ideological differences between neo-Foucauldian analysis and labor process theory with its roots in a Marxist political economy. The latter puts structurally determined class conflict at the theoretical center of any explanation regarding changing trust-control relations (Reed, 2001). Following Reed (2001, p. 211), Marxist political economy "remains grounded in a materialist analysis of the economic and political power structures which constrain the operation and redesign of organizational control regimes". Meanwhile, neo-Foucauldian analyses are committed to more open conceptions of disciplinary practices and disciplinary constructions (symbolic, linguistic) of organizational selves (ibid.). To clarify, we find inspiration primarily in Foucault's later works, the novelty of which lies in "an increasing interest in the role that the human subject plays in his or her own subordination, self-creation and self-fashioning" (Barratt, 2008, p. 516). In other words, we associate openness with assumptions of individual agency and choice supported by a positive and productive understanding of power – in contrast to the repressive negatives of disciplinary practice, domination and exploitation that tend to preoccupy critical management studies (Barratt, 2008).

Continuing on a constructive (as opposed to deconstructive) track, we turn now to the concepts of self-management and post-heroic, distributed and shared leadership and how they can serve to clarify relations between trust and control.

Post-Heroic Leadership and Self-Management

There is both a relational and an individual/subjective component to the matter of self-management – as a signifier of the tendency for managerial relations to involve an element of autonomy and self-determination on the part of the managed. The relational component is reflected in a concept such as *distributed leadership*. Distributed leadership puts focus on leadership as a relational practice as opposed to individual leaders and their knowledge, skills, roles, functions and routines. Leadership is seen as a product of the interactions of leaders and followers in particular situations (Spillane, 2005). Leadership thus appears as a shared, collective endeavor involving distributed agency. A similar pattern is suggested by the notion of *shared leadership*, a term Fletcher and Käufer (2003) use synonymously with post-heroic leadership. They use it to advocate an understanding of "leadership as a more relational process, a shared or distributed phenomenon occurring at different levels and dependent on social interactions and networks of influence" (p. 21). Leadership is thus conceptualized as "a set of practices that can and should be enacted by people at all levels rather than a set of personal characteristics and attributes located in people at the top" (p. 22). Leadership behavior and relationships are not restricted to hierarchical positions or roles but seen to occur in relational dynamics throughout an organization (Uhl-Bien, 2006), with "people work[ing] together to define and develop their relationships not just as questions of influence and leadership, but also as questions of how to keep all of this moving and working together" (Murrell, 1997, p. 40).

Fletcher and Käufer (2003) strongly emphasize the need to consider the (managerial) self-in-relation, as opposed to a self that is discrete and exists in splendid isolation from others (see also Uhl-Bien, 2006). The post-heroic ideal, following Eicher (2006), is the leader who (1) wants others to take responsibility and gain knowledge and expertise, (2) encourages innovation and participation, (3) seeks input and aims for consensus in decision-making and (4) overall wants others to grow and learn – even at the expense of himself or herself becoming dispensable (Crevani, Lindgren & Packendorf, 2007).

As mentioned in Chapter 2, post-heroic leadership can be considered as a gendered conceptualization of leadership (ibid.). Thus, it is often associated with traits that are considered as feminine or socially attributed to women, including vulnerability, empathy, care, helpfulness, interpersonal sensitivity, attentiveness to and acceptance of others, skills of inquiry and collaboration, and orientation toward the collective interest. This stands in contrast to heroic leadership traits that are culturally attributed to men or seen to reflect masculinity. These include the ability to be impersonal (and suppress emotions), toughness, objectivity, effectiveness, individualism, self-interest, assertiveness, control and domination (Fletcher, 2004; Fondas, 1997). Crevani et al. (2007) argue that post-heroic leadership tends to be associated with femininity and powerlessness and is therefore mostly invisible in organizations. However, there is bound to be contextual differences in how this plays out. Drawing on the Danish experience, we can say that post-heroic leadership developments in the form of shared or distributed leadership or self-management have actually been very visible for a number of years and have arguably not been reducible – either in theory or practice – to socially constructed gender differences.

Danish developments in the realm of "selvledelse" (self-management) can serve as an example of post-heroic leadership tendencies that, although the following treatment is admittedly very brief and very general, can bring us a little closer to practice. In Denmark, self-management has for a number of years been a favored post-bureaucratic theme. Trust-based leadership, in the context of the Danish public sector, is often considered to be a matter of creating more favorable conditions for self-management, delegation and involvement (Bentzen, 2018). Self-management has been developed theoretically (Kristensen, 2011; Kristensen & Pedersen, 2013) as well as applied in practice, particularly in the public sector. Applications range from broad principles of management and governance to self-managing groups and teams and manager-employee relationships. Apart from the realm of scholarship, these developments reflect everyday practical experience in many public sector organizations, where leadership is to some extent a matter of managing employees who, either individually or in groups, are self-managing. That is to say, they take part in determining how their own work should be carried out and have great leeway with regard to how – and sometimes where – their working hours should be spent. Even though self-management features most prominently among highly educated knowledge workers who usually have greater insight into the professional nitty-gritty of their daily work than management, its relevance is not limited to such groups. Virtually any professional endeavor in the public sector contains an element of self-management. In this particular sense, there are elements of management to be found everywhere. Responsibilities are widely distributed and shared.

Self-management can mean different things. At the most basic theoretical level, it can seem paradoxical: how can you manage people who manage themselves? How to reconcile management's (legally enshrined) right to manage with employees' expectations or demands regarding autonomy? In practice, the apparent paradox quickly dissolves. The productive view of power shows how managers can exert power while respecting the autonomy of employees and considering freedom as a resource. To iterate, power can be liberating and empowering; it does not have to be limiting and repressive.

Some associate the management of self-management with delegation of tasks, mandates and responsibility. Most managers have to delegate to make the most of available resources (not least their own), get things done and stretch their budget. Self-management is thus inextricably linked with decentralization. However, self-management can also be understood in a more fundamental and existential sort of way. Many employees – knowledge workers and others – would find it hard to imagine a work life without a high degree of freedom, autonomy and self-determination. Again, freedom does not have to be a matter of being able to determine *what* work tasks are to be carried out. It can be a matter of having significant influence on *how* they are to be carried out and how one's own time is to be prioritized in this regard. Either way, self-management is more than a functional product of delegation. It can, positively or negatively, have a significant impact on employee well-being, motivation and job satisfaction. This existential aspect is also reflected in modern notions of work as identity and medium for self-realization (Kristensen & Pedersen, 2013).

We have argued that virtually any professional endeavor in the public sector contains an element of self-management. That is certainly the case in the Danish public sector. However, there is more to self-management than emancipation, and this has been reflected in discussions about self-management in recent years. First, there is an increasing awareness that self-management is a way of thinking and practicing management – it is not a formula for laissez-faire or, if you will, managerial abstinence. Indeed, we need to talk about the *management of* self-management. Second, self-management highlights the need for dialogic and inclusive forms of management that, from the managerial point of view, do not have to be any less demanding (again, notions of distributed and shared leadership are useful to describe how such processes unfold). If self-management is to function in practice, strong agreements and ongoing dialogue are required between manager and employee(s), vis-à-vis the notion of self-in-relation. On the one hand, the employee must have some free space to assert judgment, decide and act, including some room to fail. On the other, the manager must be able to intervene when deemed necessary. Managers must trust their self-managing staff to seek advice and guidance and accept feedback when needed. Employees must ideally have some trust in the manager/management and perceive the attention paid to them as reflective of professional dialogue and follow-up rather than monitoring and control. Of course, the management of self-management is not reducible to dyadic manager-employee relationships. It also has to be considered in the context of institutional framework conditions, including collective agreements that can serve to either enable or constrain trust in self-managing relations.

Third, the freedom and autonomy we can speak of with regard to self-management is always limited, conditional and predicated on responsibility.

It is not a license to act freely with no strings attached, without consideration of significant others and the organizational context. Self-management is predicated on individual or collective willingness and ability to make a contribution supporting the objectives of the organization. It requires an ability to see your own effort as part of a larger organizational whole or a larger community. Freedom is thus always predicated on responsibility in relation to organizational objectives (Kristensen, 2011; Kristensen & Pedersen, 2013).

Fourth, self-management can be both inclusive and excluding. Self-management, to function properly, presupposes a certain level of trust and thus a forging of social relations. Self-management can be demanding, especially for employees who are saddled with more responsibility in the sense that they are expected not only to do a particular job but also to take part in, using the vocabulary of CMS, engineering and reengineering identities and roles as they relate to work tasks, work boundaries and measures of (self-)evaluation. Self-managing employees are expected to give more of their engaged selves to the organization. In return, they should ideally get a greater sense of recognition, identity and purpose out of their employment. However, there can also be an excluding downside to the self-management imperative. In organizations that work explicitly with self-management, there seems to be less and less room left for non-self-managing employees. That is, employees who may be keen to do their usual jobs and serve their usual functions, but find it difficult to live up to requirements regarding self-reflective self-determination and -development in the workplace – for example, experienced staff members doing routine operational work. With the focus on self-management, there is a tendency for operational staff to be excluded in favor of self-realizing self-developers.

In sum, self-management can in some instances appear to be a turbo-charged individualization of responsibility. Mind you, not just responsibility for one self, but also responsibility for organizational performance. While management of self-management presupposes trust, it is important that trust-based leadership does not become a carte blanche for delegating mandates and responsibilities to already hardworking middle managers and employees. This again points to the relevance of the array of concerns regarding domination and control raised by CMS scholarship.

Trust and Values

Yet another post-bureaucratic theme worth mentioning is values and values-based management, which is part of the culture and identity lineage in management theory and practice and associable with Weberian notions of value rationality. Values-based management is meant to replace rules with values – or rather, it is meant to complement rule-based governance with values-based governance (Jørgensen, 2003, 2006). Values are important for a number of reasons. First, modern public organizations want to signal their adherence to strong human and social values that amount to more than compliance with existing rules and regulations, economic responsibility and delivery of good and dependable public service. They want to be associated with values such as trust, responsibility, integrity, respect, diversity and sustainability. Second, values are supposed to be more flexible and open to interpretation than rules, and therefore they can empower public employees in situations characterized by high uncertainty, where action is called for and rules do not suffice. Third, (shared) values are associated with the creation of organizational communities (Knudsen, 2004).

Although trust is one of the most often used value-words, such value articulation is, in itself, an inadequate placeholder for trust. One reason being that values, in many organizations, are more a matter of talk than action. Building on the Danish experience, we do acknowledge that there are organizations that deserve to be called genuinely values-based and - governed, but generally speaking, it appears as if values-based management is no longer very fashionable. Many articulated values statements tend to be taken for granted and to have lost managerial capital. Therefore, it is important to understand trust as more than an aspect of values-based management. Many middle managers in (formally) values-based organizations experience that they lead with trust while themselves encountering distrust from above in the organization – and that there is often a considerable gap between talk and action when it comes to espoused values. In many organizations, values are taken for granted and met with indifference and perhaps disappointment. Under these conditions, trust-based leadership needs to be more than a matter of breathing new life into the rather worn-out value-word "trust". It is important not to assume that trust is a shared value – considering the challenges that are involved in creating and maintaining trust. What we advocate is a more tangible and action-oriented agenda that aims to build on and strengthen social relations in organizations.

One trust-based critique of organizational uses of values has to do with their embedding into systems of governance. In some organizations, values effectively function as rules – in the sense that they are subject to ongoing monitoring, measurement and evaluation of the extent to which managers and employees live up to them. In such cases, values are no longer something positive that is meant to motivate and guide action, but rather something negative that is associable with control and threat of sanctions. This can lead to hypocrisy about values (enforced lip service) and is not conducive to the general idea that values should make a positive contribution to people's sense of meaning and identification with the organization. However, attitudes toward and experiences of values are bound to differ, and we cannot generally say that values-based management and trust-based management cannot work together and mutually support one another. In some public organizations, they appear to be natural extensions of one another. Whereas some organizations are characterized by what we may term *value cynicism*, others are characterized by *value idealism*. If people experience that orientation toward values makes a positive difference in their daily work and is something that organizational members act on and are committed to, it can support the building of trust (or, conversely, the feeling that you have to resort to hypocrisy if you cannot "feel" the values that give meaning to others around you).

Trust, Power and Motivation

Finally, in this chapter, we turn to the matter of motivation and how it is interwoven with trust and power in a public sector context. We have already discussed how our chosen approach intersects with and differs from critical management studies. Turning to motivation allows us to, once again, show how our view differs from approaches rooted in the economic paradigm. The relevant literature on motivation is thus based on economic assumptions about human behavior. Management and governance relations are construed as principal-agent relations involving information asymmetry, opportunism and moral hazard, while the question of trust is relegated to the background (see Chapter 2). The problem addressed by this literature is not a lack of trust *per se*, but rather the realization that economic governance does not always work as intended and can even be counterproductive because it conflicts with the norms and values that motivate public sector employees (Andersen & Pedersen, 2014). As we have argued, the economic perspective favors distrust over trust (or system trust over social trust) and encounters difficulties when it comes to accommodating the positive value of (social) trust. However, it can be helpful in providing a more nuanced account of how trust is related to motivation and built into public governance.

A key concept in the literature on motivation is PSM: *public service motivation*. It is a particular form of altruistic motivation associated with warm hands, care and doing good for others (people in need) and for society. PSM overlaps with intrinsic motivation, which is related to the work task itself (what it means to do a good job and be a skilled professional) and need not have anything to do with regard for others. Both differ from extrinsic motivation, which stems from external rewards and punishment, carrots and sticks. In practice, most public employees will be motivated by a combination of intrinsic and extrinsic factors (Le Grand, 2010). Of particular interest, for present purposes, is what happens when assumptions about motivation intersect with principles and practices of governance.

The anthropology of trust is characterized by optimism. Focus is on the value of benevolence and reciprocity in social relations. This anthropology is well aligned with the altruistic notion of PSM, but contemporary managerial understandings of what drives public sector employees tend to be much less optimistic overall. Le Grand (2003, 2010) divides public employees into two ideal types, *knights* and *knaves*, and argues that they call for different forms of governance. While knights are characterized by a high degree of PSM, knaves are transactional and selfish optimizers of their own utility. Knaves want to optimize the relationship between contribution and benefit: to work as little as they can get away with and get as much out of their minimal effort as possible. Whereas knights are driven by an inner work ethic and strong values, knaves adhere to extrinsic forms of motivation: economic incentives and the risk of punishment. With regard to the primacy of distrust over trust, notice how both categories are described in a way that calls for control: it is necessary to curb the altruistic and caring inclinations of knights as they would otherwise drive up costs, and knaves are obviously not deserving of trust.

The unbalanced or simplified (in our view) understanding of trust in Le Grand's conceptualization comes to the fore in his transfer of the categories of knights and knaves to models of public governance. Based on the UK experience, he describes the development of two service models that he calls "trust" and "mistrust", respectively. His outline of the former model illustrates the categorical mistake of associating trust with an absence of governance and thus pure and undiluted professional autonomy. In the trust model, according to Le Grand, public employees, doctors, nurses, teachers and social workers are driven by PSM and thus concern for the common good and people's welfare. We can therefore trust these knights to deliver quality services without direct interference from the state or others. The basic idea being that it is the professionals who actually deliver public services who are best positioned to allocate scarce resources and ensure efficiency, continuous development, responsibility and high quality. Furthermore, this is supposed to work best when public services are not exposed to competition and market pressures or made subject to economic incentives – as such forces can have a corrupting influence on the proper intrinsic motivation of public sector managers and employees (Le Grand, 2010).

The problem with this model, according to Le Grand (and we agree), is that it has proven ineffective in practice. It has made it difficult to implement new policies, ensure capacity to change and boost quality in the public sector. Torfing (quoted in Siegumfeldt, 2016) has observed that in Denmark in the early 1980s, when the first experiments with NPM were made, the public sector suffered from absolutist rule by the professions. Strong and entitled professional groups stood guard over their fields of expertise, methods and budgets, and were opposed to all innovation, tone deaf to political signals and paternalistic in their treatment of citizens. The "mistrust" model has subsequently proven to be a more effective way to generate measurable results and development in areas like health and education. It can take different forms, but the model is broadly associated with top-down governance, supported by NPM-inspired governance and management tools and a layer of lawyers and economists who treat everybody from top to bottom as knaves. Instead of trust, the focus is on provision of effective incentives – carrots and sticks – to ensure that managers and employees are motivated and work toward shared goals (Le Grand, 2010).

According to this framing, mistrust wins over trust. It is preferable to consider all public employees as knaves than to rely on their knightly benevolence. Mistrust generates better results – at least of the measurable kind. That is the message. But there is something wrong with this grand narrative. While it describes how NPM has become a winning formula for public governance, it misrepresents what the contemporary trust agenda is all about.

Trust, in our view, is not a nostalgic endeavor aiming to return public sector organizations to a time before the advent of NPM when professions and professional self-regulation reigned supreme. Trust, as we have argued at length, is not about managerial abstinence and absence of governance and external controls in favor of professional autonomy. If it was, its claim to practical relevance would be very limited indeed. The underlying ideal is not a return to how things used to be in the past, but rather the active making of a present and a future marked by smarter and more effective balancing of trust, power and control.

Le Grand's framing is arguably reflective of the previously mentioned tendency in political science to define trust as naïve and unconditional while considering skepticism and distrust as positives (Six, 2013). It is also, arguably, reflective of the tendency to give institutional and, in particular, economic trust the cognitive and rational upper hand compared to, in this case, professional attachments to times gone by. It represents categorical economic thinking that is well suited for large quantitative studies of public employees' motivations, but less capable when it comes to addressing qualitative and relational aspects of management and governance. In general, there is a tendency for the literature on governance and motivation to downplay the process perspective and the performative aspects of categorization (i.e., how categories not only reflect an underlying reality, but also partake in creating social reality through their use).

This is not to say that the notion of the knave is exclusively a product of economic theory. Negative perceptions of public employees as lazy and untrustworthy are common among professionals (internally) and in public debate (externally), and may be based on prejudice as well as experience (see Chapter 4 on othering). However, such negative perceptions among professionals (principals) can be partly attributable to the performative and stereotyping effect of economic models assuming opportunistic and self-serving behavior on the part of agents. The question is whether we by reducing employees to such stereotypes run the risk of pigeonholing them and creating a self-fulfilling prophecy. Le Grand's message is clear: we cannot afford trust, and mistrust creates better results. It is a political-ideological statement that serves to legitimize the tools and powers of NPM and, as we have argued, there can be a tendency for mistrust to be self-fulfilling: if you meet others with mistrust, you will often get paid in kind.

In other words, there is a need to reflect on categories like knights and knaves, or rather the tools of management and governance they are manifest in, and how they influence the managers and employees who are subject to them. Although the literature on governance and motivation does acknowledge that you can make knaves out of public employees by treating them like knaves, and that the resulting lack of trust may result in lower motivation, it fails to take the full consequence of this insight. That is, it fails to embrace trust as part of possible forward-looking solutions. It is, of course, difficult to embrace trust if you, like Le Grand, associate it with the absence of governance rather than the presence of management.

Motivation Crowding

The need to address questions about process and performativity is, to some extent, met by the theories and analyses surrounding the concept of *motivation crowding* (Frey, 1994, 1997; Frey & Jegen, 2000). Discussions of motivation crowding underline the importance of how managers and employees experience and ascribe meaning to the modes of management and governance they are subjected to. What matters is not (only) the form of management or governance in itself, but how it is decoded on the receiving end. We touched upon this problematic earlier in the chapter, when we addressed the matter of whether control is perceived as meaningful or not. Motivation crowding constitutes a formalization of this argument, but only addresses the question of trust indirectly.

Motivation crowding primarily serves to illustrate the point that economic incentives can undermine people's inner/intrinsic motivation to carry out a task. In social psychology, this mechanism is referred to as "the hidden costs of reward" (Frey, 1997; Frey & Jegen, 2000). For present purposes, it has particular relevance as yet another way to challenge the economic principles that underpin NPM. There are two different mechanisms at play here: the "crowding-out" effect and the "crowding-in" effect. The former represents a significant anomaly in modern economic thinking: that greater economic incentives in some instances can have an adverse effect on supply (Frey & Jegen, 2000). When social relations and transactions that have not otherwise relied on economic payment become monetized, this can lead to lower motivation for the involved parties (an often mentioned example of this is the expected negative effects of introducing monetary rewards for organ donation). The important point is that management and governance practices that are based on economic models can have the effect of weakening or destroying the noneconomic aspects of organization (Ariely, 2008; Gneezy & Rustichini, 2000), including people's intrinsic motivation and social relations between organizational members (Frey & Jegen, 2000; Gibbons, 1998). Conversely, the crowding-in effect suggests that economic incentives (and other forms of extrinsic motivation) can be supportive of people's intrinsic motivation (Frey & Jegen, 2000).

According to principal-agent theory, external intervention in the form of economic incentives or regulation will either increase the cost of underperforming or increase the marginal economic benefit of doing good work. We can refer to this as a relative price effect that can serve to discipline behavior. Economic theory most often assumes this disciplinary effect while neglecting the importance of intrinsic motivation. The reason for this neglect is that it is difficult, if not impossible, to determine exactly the composition of an employee's internal and external motivations for doing a job. It is easier to articulate and assess the effects of a number of directly observable extrinsic motivators (Frey & Jegen, 2000).

The problem is, however, that extrinsic motivation (in the form of positive economic incentives or regulations imposing negative sanctions) can have either a positive or a negative effect on employees' intrinsic motivation. If extrinsic motivation is associated with limited autonomy and self-determination, and lack of recognition of the individual's commitment and qualifications, this can lead to a crowding-out effect. This occurs when the management or governance that people are subjected to is experienced as *controlling*. Conversely, a crowding-in effect can occur when management or governance is perceived as *supportive* and people feel they are treated with respect and left with more freedom to act and greater self-determination (Deci & Ryan, 2012; Frey & Jegen, 2000). DeHart-Davis (2008) refers to such meaningful rules and controls as enabling *green tape*.

Although motivation crowding only indirectly promotes trust as a solution (vis-à-vis the economic trust paradigm's strained relationship with social trust), its contribution to the trust agenda lies in its articulation of how management and governance need to be perceived as positive and supportive (vis-à-vis our earlier discussion of productive power) if they are to have a positive effect on people's intrinsic motivation and create a crowding-in effect. On a more moderate, some would say more realistic, note, it is important for management not to be perceived as controlling if it is to capitalize on trusting relations. The main takeaway from this discussion is that economic governance can be counterproductive and turn out to have perverse effects if it is perceived to violate public employees' sense of self-esteem and experienced self-determination. Knightly altruists can turn into cynics – if not outright knaves – if they feel they are met with mistrust (Frey, 1997; Le Grand, 2010). At the same time, we cannot disregard the need for economic governance and accountability. Motivation crowding alerts us to how, for example, economic incentives can have both controlling and supporting effects. This brings us back to the point that control and the tools of economic governance can be both repressive and productive, and that one of the challenges of trust-based leadership is to operationalize control in such a way so that it becomes a productive and if not motivating then certainly not demotivating force. The aim is to enhance possibilities of a crowding-in effect and accomplish a symbiotic relationship between trust and control (Edelenbos & Eshuis, 2012).

After this engagement with the economic literature on motivation, we will resume our outline of the relational paradigm by turning to developments in social capital and thus the aspects of post-bureaucratic thinking that have to do with community.

References

Adler, P. S. (2012). The sociological ambivalence of bureaucracy: From Weber via Gouldner to Marx. *Organization Science*, 23, 244–266.

Andersen, L. B. & Pedersen, L. H. (2014). *Styring og motivation i den offentlige sektor*. [Governance and motivation in the public sector]. Tilst: Jurist- og Økonomforbundets Forlag.

Ariely, D. (2008). *Predictably irrational*. St. Ives: Harper.

Bachmann, R. (2001). Trust, power and control in trans-organizational relations. *Organization Studies*, 22(2), 337–365.

Barley, S. & Kunda, G. (1992). Design and devotion: Surges of rational and normative ideologies of control in managerial discourse. *Administrative Science Quarterly*, 37, 363–399.

Barratt, E. (2008). The later Foucault in organization and management studies. *Human Relations*, 61(4), 515–537.

Bentzen, T. Ø. (2018). *Tillidsbaseret styring og ledelse i offentlige organisationer.* [Trust-based governance and management in public organizations]. Højbjerg: Jurist- og Økonomforbundets Forlag.

Bradach, J. L. & Eccles, R. G. (1989). Price, authority, trust and control: From ideal types to plural forms. *American Review of Sociology*, 15, 97–118.

Braverman, H. (1974). *Labor and monopoly capital.* New York: Monthly Review Press.

Bijlsma-Frankema, K. & Costa, A. C. (2005). Understanding the trust-control nexus. *International Sociology*, 20(3), 259–282.

Costa, A. C. & Bijlsma-Frankema, K. (2007). Trust and control interrelations – New perspectives on the trust-control nexus. *Group & Organization Management*, 32(4), 392–406.

Crevani, L., Lindgren, M. & Packendorff, J. (2007). Shared leadership: A postheroic perspective on leadership as a collective construction. *International Journal of Leadership Studies*, 3(1), 40–67.

Dahl, R. A. (1957). The concept of power. *Systems Research and Behavioral Science*, 2(3), 201–215.

Das, T. K. & Teng, B.-S. (1998). Between trust and control: Developing confidence in partner cooperation in alliances. *The Academy of Management Review*, 23(3), 491–512.

Deci, E. L. & Ryan, R. M. (2012). Self-determination theory. In P. A. M. Van Lange, A. W. Kruglanski & E. T. Higgins (Eds.). *Handbook of theories of social psychology* (416–436). Thousand Oaks, CA: Sage.

Deetz, S. (1995). *Transforming communication, transforming business: Building responsive and responsible workplaces.* Cresskill, NJ: Hampton Press.

DeHart-Davis, L. (2008). Green tape: A theory of effective organizational rules. *Journal of Public Administration Research and Theory*, 19(2), 361–384.

Edelenbos, J. & Eshuis, J. (2012). The interplay between trust and control in governance processes: A conceptual and empirical investigation. *Administration & Society*, 44(6), 647–674.

Eicher, J. P. (2006). *Post-heroic leadership: Managing the virtual organization.* Retrieved from www.pignc-ispi.com/articles/management/post-heroic.htm

Eisenstadt, S. N. (1959). Bureaucracy, bureaucratization, and debureaucratization. *Administrative Science Quarterly*, 4(3), 302–320.

Ettlinger, N. (2011). Governmentality as epistemology. Annals of the *Association of American Geographers*, 101(3), 537–560.

Faubion, J. D. (Ed.) (1994). *Power. Essential works of Foucault 1954–1984.* New York: The New Press.

Fleming, P. & Spicer, A. (2003). Working at a cynical distance: Implications for power, subjectivity and resistance. *Organization*, 10(1), 157–179.

Fletcher, J. K. (2004). The paradox of postheroic leadership: An essay on gender, power, and transformational change. *The Leadership Quarterly*, 15(5), 647–661.

Fletcher, J. K. & Käufer, K. (2003). Shared leadership: Paradox and possibility. Ch. 2 in C. L. Pearce & J. A. Conger (Eds.). *Shared leadership: Reframing the hows and whys of leadership* (21–47). Thousand Oaks, CA: Sage.

Fondas, N. (1997). Feminization unveiled: Management qualities in contemporary writing. *Academy of Management Review*, 22(1), 257–282.

Foucault, M. (1977). *Discipline and punish. The birth of the prison*. London: Penguin Books.

Foucault, M. (1978). Governmentality. In J. D. Faubion (Ed.) (1994). *Power. Essential works of Foucault 1954–1984* (201–222). New York: The New Press.

Foucault, M. (1980). Truth and power. In J. D. Faubion (Ed.) (1994). *Power. Essential works of Foucault 1954–1984* (111–133). New York: The New Press.

Foucault, M. (1982). The subject and power. In J. D. Faubion (Ed.) (1994). *Power. Essential works of Foucault 1954–1984* (326–348). New York: The New Press.

Foucault, M. (2009). *Security, territory, population – Lectures at Collège de France 1977–1978*. Hampshire: Palgrave MacMillan.

Fournier, V. (1999). The appeal to professionalism as a disciplinary mechanism. *The Sociological Review*, 47(2), 280–307.

Frey, B. (1994). How intrinsic motivation is crowded out and in. *Rationality & Society*, 6(3), 334–352.

Frey, B. (1997). A constitution for knaves crowds out civic virtues. *Economic Journal*, 107(443), 1043–1053.

Frey, B. & Jegen, R. (2000). *Motivation crowding theory: A survey of empirical evidence*, CESifo Working Paper, No. 245, Ifo Institute – Leibniz Institute for Economic Research at the University of Munich.

Fuglsang, L. & Jagd, S. (2013). Making sense of institutional trust in organizations: Bridging institutional context and trust. *Organization*, 22(1), 23–39.

Gibbons, R. (1998). Incentives in organizations. *Journal of Economic Perspectives*, 12, 115–132.

Gioia, D. & Chittipeddi, K. (1991). Sensemaking and sensegiving in strategic change initiation. *Strategic Management Journal*, 12(6), 433–448.

Gneezy, U. & Rustichini, A. (2000). A fine is a prize. *Journal of Legal Studies*, XXIX, 1–17.

Grey, C. & Garsten, C. (2001). Trust, control and post-bureaucracy. *Organization Studies*, 22(2), 229–250.

Hartman, L. (Ed.) (2011). *Konkurrensens konsekvenser: Vad händer med svensk välfärd*. [Consequences of competition: What is happening to Swedish welfare]. Stockholm, Sweden: SNS Forlag.

Heckscher, C. (1994). Defining the post- bureaucratic type. In C. Heckscher & A. Donnellon (Eds.). *The Post-bureaucratic organization: New perspectives on organizational change* (14–62). Thousand Oaks, CA: Sage.

Hodgson, D. E. (2004). Project work: The legacy of bureaucratic control in the postbureaucratic organization. *Organization*, 11(1), 81–100.

Hood, C. & Dixon, R. (2015). *A government that worked better and cost less? Evaluating three decades of reform and change in UK central government*. Oxford: Oxford University Press.

Jagd, S. (2009). Tillidsbaseret ledelse – en ny udfordring for ledere. *Ledelse & Erhvervsøkonomi*, 3, 7–21.

Jørgensen, T. B. (2003). *På sporet af en offentlig identitet – værdier i stat, amter og kommuner*. [On the trail of a public identity – values in the state, regions and municipalities]. Aarhus: Aarhus Universitetsforlag.

Jørgensen, T. B. (2006). Value consciousness and public management. *International Journal of Organization and Behavior*, 9(4), 510–536.

Kamp, A., Hohnen, P., Hvid, H. & Scheller, V. K. (2013). *New public management – Konsekvenser for arbejdsmiljø og produktivitet*. [New public management –

Consequences for work environment and productivity]. Roskilde Universitet, Skriftserie for Center For Arbejdslivsforskning, Nr. 3. http://rossy.ruc.dk/ojs/index.php/caf/article/view/3061

Khodyakov, D. (2007). Trust as a process: A three-dimensional approach. *Sociology*, 41(1), 115–132.

Knudsen, H. (2004). Licens til kritik – og andre måder at bruge værdier på i organisationer. [License to critique – and other ways of using values in organizations]. In D. Pedersen (Ed.). *Offentlig ledelse i managementstaten* [Public management in the management state] (159–175). København: Samfundslitteratur.

Kristensen, A. R. (2011). *Det grænseløse arbejdsliv. Om at lede de selvledende medarbejdere.* [The limitless work life. On managing self-managing employees]. Aarhus: Gyldendal Business.

Kristensen, A. R. & Pedersen, M. (2013). *Strategisk selvledelse. Ledelse mellem frihed og forretning.* [Strategic self-management. Management between freedom and business]. Riga: Gyldendal Business.

Kroeger, F. (2019). Unlocking the treasure trove: How can Luhmann's theory of trust enrich trust research? *Journal of Trust Research*, 9(1), 110–124.

Kunda, G. (1992). *Engineering culture: Control and commitment in a high-tech corporation.* Philadelphia, PA: Temple University Press.

Le Grand, J. (2003). *Motivation, agency, and public policy: Of knights and knaves, pawns and queens.* Oxford: Oxford University Press.

Le Grand, J. (2010). Knights and knaves return: Public service motivation and the delivery of public services. *International Public Management Journal*, 13(1), 56–71.

Long, C. P. & Sitkin, S. B. (2006). Trust in the balance: How managers integrate trust-building and task control. In R. Bachmann & A. Zaheer (Eds.). *Handbook of trust research* (87–106). Cornwall: Edward Elgar.

Luhmann, N. (2017). *Trust and power.* St. Ives: Polity Press.

Lukes, S. (1974). *Power: A radical view.* Hong Kong: MacMillan Education.

Lund, H. L., Hvid, H., Nielsen, K. T., Kamp, A. & Nielsen, K. A. (2008). *Fleksibilitet på godt og ondt.* [Flexibility, for better worse]. København: FTF dokumentation.

Maravelias, C. (2003). Post-bureaucracy – Control through professional freedom. *Journal of Organizational Change Management*, 16(5), 547–566.

Melander, P. (Ed.) (2008). *Det fortrængte offentlige lederskab. Offentlig ledelse efter new public management.* [Displacement of public leadership: Public management after New Public Management]. Gylling: Jurist- og Økonomforbundets Forlag.

Monteiro, P. & Adler, P. S. (2022). Bureaucracy for the 21st century: Clarifying and expanding our view of bureaucratic organization. *Academy of Management Annals.* Preprint version. https://doi.org/10.5465/annals.2019.0059

Möllering, G. (2005). The trust/control duality. *International Sociology*, 20(3), 283–305.

Murrell, K. L. (1997). Emergent theories of leadership for the next century: Towards relational concepts. *Organization Development Journal*, 15(3), 35–42.

Olsen, J. P. (2008). The ups and downs of bureaucratic organization. *Annual Review of Political Science*, 11, 13–37.

Produktivitetskommissionen. (2014). *Det handler om velstand og velfærd. Slutrapport.* [About prosperity and welfare (Final report)]. København: Produktivitetskommissionen.

Reed, M. I. (2001). Organization, trust and control: A realist analysis. *Organization Studies*, 22(2), 201–228.

Siegumfeldt, P. (2016). Kommuner gør op med new public management. *Akademikerbladet*, Nr. 9. www.akademikerbladet.dk/magasinet/2016/magisterbladet-nr-9-2016/kommuner-goer-op-med-new-public-management

Siltala, J. (2013). New public management: The evidence-based worst practice? *Administration & Society*, 45(4), 468–493.

Six, F. (2013). Trust in regulatory relations: How new insights from trust research improve regulation theory. *Public Management Review*, 15(2), 163–185.

Spillane, J. P. (2005). Distributed leadership. *The Educational Forum*, 69(2), 143–150.

Sprenger, R. K. (2004). *Trust. The best way to manage.* London: Cyan/Campus.

Sydow, J. (1998). Understanding the constitution of interorganizational trust. In C. Lane & R. Bachmann (Eds.). *Trust within and between organizations* (31–63). Oxford: Oxford University Press.

Sztompka, P. (1999). *Trust – A sociological theory.* Cambridge: Cambridge University Press.

Uhl-Bien, M. (2006). Relational leadership theory: Exploring the social processes of leadership and organizing. *Leadership Quarterly*, 17, 654–676.

Vallentin, S. & Thygesen, N. (2017). Trust and control in public sector reform: Complementary and beyond. *Journal of Trust Research*, 7(2), 150–169.

Weibel, A. (2007). Formal control and trustworthiness – Shall the twain never meet. *Group & Organization Management*, 32(4), 500–517.

4 Social Capital and the Gift Economy

In this chapter we engage with the concept of social capital and the managerial and organizational practices associated herewith. The justifications for this are both theoretical and empirical. Theoretically, social capital has obvious affinities with trust, as trust is a key component in most definitions of what social capital is or does. Under this heading we find promotion of social cohesion and inclusiveness – as opposed to hierarchical division of labor or market-based disaggregation and competition. The ideal is organizations characterized by goodwill, benevolence and reciprocity in social relations – in support of employee well-being and sense of belonging, collaboration, coordination and performance.

This means, on the one hand, that social capital has important contributions to make to our theoretical framing and understanding of public sector trust. To focus on social capital is one way to convey a more tangible and hands-on, even structural, sense of what it means to create or strive toward creating the relational organization (Osborne, 2006). On the other, we have to be aware of issues of power, conflicting interests and difference in relation to social capital (vis-à-vis our reflections in Chapter 3), as such issues tend to be brushed aside in this discourse. In other words, we have to be aware of resulting power deficits and reflect on the dark sides (or potential dark sides) of organizational social capital. Importantly, social capital takes us beyond the inner workings of public organizations and dyadic relationships as it (also) embraces a larger ecosystem of possible collaboration, co-creation, partnerships and networked forms of governance (Klijn & Koppenjan, 2016) involving separate organizational entities. While trust is an important antecedent for collaboration between public organizations and other actors to take place, "Social Capital" can be a call to arms supporting such collaboration across silos.

Apart from an interest in theorizing social capital, both in terms of its explicit ("Social Capital") and implicit manifestations, we also want to support a managerial understanding of how it can serve as a lever for trust-based development within and between public sector organizations (and other actors). To focus on social capital is one way to enable the trust agenda and turn it into a matter of addressing and experimenting with relationship building within and between public organizations. As we shall see

DOI: 10.4324/9780429431104-4

(Chapter 5), this potential has been clearly articulated and acted upon as part of the Danish trust reform.

This in turn points to the empirical reality of social capital in public organizations and thus the matter of how our approach finds support in practical applications. Speaking from the Danish experience, and going back to our earlier point about the double hermeneutic of social science (Chapter 1), the enactment of trust in the Danish public sector has to a large extent, in many organizations, taken place within the frame of "Social Capital". Hence, the "Social Capital" agenda with attendant tools and practices came into being and was well-established before the trust agenda became a thing and was acknowledged in its own right. "Social Capital" has over the last 10–15 years emerged as a very active and influential agenda with strong political and organizational support – based on a shared interest in building strong working environments and supporting employee well-being and performance (in that order). Based on the work of Peter Hasle and colleagues (Hasle, Thoft & Olesen, 2010; Olesen et al., 2008), initially under the auspices of NFA – the National Research Centre for the Working Environment, efforts to strengthen "Social Capital" in and around public organizations have become institutionalized in a particular operational definition (combining the variables of *Trust, Ability to collaborate* and *Justice*) and a particular set of practices (*Bonding, Bridging* and *Linking*), along with its own metrics and means of quantification (standardized employee surveys). As Portes (2000) points out, the theoretical problems involved in establishing the meaning and relational properties of social capital can be partially compensated by efforts to measure it empirically. Discussions of social capital's relational properties can thus be replaced with methodology and surveys of individuals' experiences and points of view (Szreter & Woolcock, 2003) – allowing managers and consultants to cut through the complexity with numbers and graphs. Notwithstanding the operational benefits of such replacement, we find it imperative, as part of the narrative of this book, to maintain a relational understanding of social capital and take up this conceptual challenge (instead of giving the impression, with surveys, that social capital is a property of individuals).

As indicated, the "Social Capital" agenda is reflecting shared interests, material concerns and mobilization among a number of influential actors, including leadership of public organizations, trade unions and consultancies. It is centered on the win-win of social well-being and performance and explicitly aims to support the creation and maintenance of good psychological working environments. Moreover, "Social Capital" lends itself more easily to commodification than does trust as it provides a more focused, circumscribed and goal-oriented set of starting points. "Social Capital" has indeed been made into a product, a deliverable that you can bring in consultants to help work on and improve, sometimes occasioned by a burning platform evoked by negative employee well-being surveys or other types of negative feedback. The fact that "Social Capital" is equipped with its own means of quantification and measurement lends it an air of organizational integration: It is something that can be measured and acted upon on an ongoing basis, alongside other issues pertaining to the working environment.

Our investment in these empirical developments is dual. On the one hand, we see no reason to reinvent the wheel as far the managerial understanding of organizational social capital goes. The prior discourse provides a solid basis for framing and engaging with the relevant types of relationships. On the other, we do see a need to clarify the rules of engagement with regard to the underlying theoretical understanding of social capital as such. On top of that, we want to expand the discussion of social capital through the use of social exchange theory focusing on the workings of gift exchange and the gift economy. We find that the focus on the gift and giving is a useful way to crystalize and bring to the fore not only the fundamentals of social capital and relational thinking, but also important aspects of trust-based leadership. Along the way, however, we want to challenge blind spots, exclusions and taken for granted notions of the social capital discourse by addressing, again, issues of power, conflicts of interests and difference. One important issue of difference has to do with diversity and how the social capital discourse tends to assume a certain sameness among social actors, thereby disregarding cultural barriers to inclusion and the achievement of shared values. We address this issue by focusing on the problem of *othering* and how social capital, at least potentially, can be a way to address and remedy problems of othering in modern organizations. We proceed to set the scene through a discussion of the fundamentals of the concept of social capital and the caveats of applying it in an organizational context.

Social Capital – Concept and Caveats

The concept of social capital is a product of the discipline of sociology, where it is used to underpin analyses of (1) the value of individuals' social networks; (2) relationship building on a collective level – in social communities; or, albeit to a lesser extent, (3) combinations of both (Adler & Kwon, 2002; Lin, 2001). Social capital is one of sociology's great "export successes" (Portes, 2000; Portes & Vickstrom, 2011) and has in recent years matured from a mere concept into a field of research that has been described as a "growth industry" (Baker & Faulkner, 2009; Kwon & Adler, 2014). However, the ways in which the concept is put to use in public discourse and utilized by other academic disciplines, including management and organization studies, is often met with skepticism among sociologists. Popular and/or instrumental approaches to social capital tend to focus primarily on the positive and normatively desirable aspects of the concept, thus sacrificing analytical precision in favor of concrete guidelines and prescriptions for action. These tendencies tend to prevail when social capital is understood on a collective level (Lin, 2001).

Portes (2000) speaks of how social capital is often turned into "an unmitigated celebration of community" (p. 10), and how "it risks becoming synonymous with each and all things that are positive in social life" (p. 3). He argues that it is indeed this celebration of community that has made the concept attractive to other disciplines and has created a buzz around it in public discourse. However, the celebratory tone sustaining the rise and proliferation of social capital and community ideals of organization is not unproblematic. One problem, Portes (2000) argues, is that causes and effects of social capital as a collective trait are often not disentangled, resulting in circular reasoning. At the individual level, the causes of social capital are attributed to a person's network, while effects are seen to be material and informational benefits. Collective social capital lacks this separation, and as a result the argument often becomes quite self-evidently positive. As a property of organizations, social capital is said to lead to better and more effective management and governance while its existence is at the same time inferred from these same outcomes (paraphrasing Portes, 2000). Social capital becomes both cause and effect, and the result is a tautological argument that is closed to critical reflection.

A related problem has to do with the political interest in embracing social capital as an unequivocal social good, and how research wittingly or unwittingly lends support to such one-sided positivity. Portes (1998) argues that the research literature, with its sociological bias, have its eyes set on how good things can emerge from sociability, while bad things are associated with behaviors of homo economicus and thus perils of capitalism (vis-à-vis our critique of the economic trust paradigm). This bias in turn reflects a critical view of "the growing power of market and hierarchy relative to community in capitalist society" (Adler, Kwon & Heckscher, 2008, p. 363). However, in keeping with Portes, there are also obvious downsides to social capital that need to be addressed – in order to stay within the realm of serious sociological analysis and avoid moralizing statements. Downsides include exclusion of outsiders (barring others from access to resources), restrictions on individual freedoms (demands for conformity as a form of social control), and downward-levelling norms (driven by an oppositional "us" vs. "them" stance). The mafia and other forms of organized crime are emblematic of how embeddedness in social structures can lead to undesirable social ends (Portes, 1998). Kwon and Adler (2014, p. 418) speak of social capital's "capacity to fragment broader collectivities in the name of local, particularistic identities". With Portes and Vickstrom (2011) they argue that this dark side (and associated risks) too often have been treated as an afterthought and not as fundamental to any discussion of social capital. We address the more mundane organizational ramifications of these downsides later in the chapter.

A third concern has to do with context and contextual differences. Sociological approaches to social capital are preoccupied with the workings of social relationships, networks and communities within a civil society context (Nahapiet & Ghoshal, 1998), sometimes with a particular focus on the significance of political institutions and the state (Rothstein & Stolle, 2008). Needless to say, empirical findings and theory development relating to a societal level of analysis are not immediately applicable to organizational settings. Unlike social communities, where the actors are formally equals (or at least can be assumed to be), organizations are hierarchical systems with asymmetrical power relations between managers and employees, superiors and subordinates. Nevertheless, there is tendency for social capital to the translated from one context to another without much reflection on differences between the two. The point being that applying social capital to modern organizations calls for reflection on how such translations are made. With these caveats in mind (and to be revisited), we will now engage more productively with social capital and how it can be helpful in making the value and structural configurations of relational trust more tangible.

Social Capital and the Relational Paradigm

Trust has its own social economy, and the concept of social capital is useful as a means to describe its rules of engagement. Using this concept takes us into a neo-capital discourse where new and extended uses are made of the language of economics. This makes it possible to distinguish between different forms of capital (Lin, 2001): *economic capital* (money, material goods), *physical capital* (buildings, machinery, tools), *human or intellectual capital* (education, knowledge, qualifications), *natural capital* (natural resources, land and ecosystems) and *social capital*, which refers to the value of social relationships among individual and/or collective actors. The prevalence and worth of social capital imply that organizations are not reducible to hierarchies, markets or technical production systems (Adler & Kwon, 2002). They are also social worlds, and their social functioning is intertwined with their ability to perform (see Ariely, 2008, Chapter 4). To clarify, when engaging with social *capital* we are highlighting qualities of the relational paradigm, not surrendering to the economic trust paradigm as outlined in Chapter 2. With social capital comes a strong emphasis on norms and values regarding goodwill, benevolence and reciprocity (Dolfsma, van der Eijk & Jolink, 2009; Portes, 1998; Putnam, 1995). This contrasts with the negative assumptions about human behavior that sustain New Public Management (NPM). In our critical treatment of NPM, we have argued that market norms (as manifestations of extrinsic motivation) can undermine social norms (as in crowding out of intrinsic motivation). Efforts to support social capital in public organizations are meant to strengthen social norms and create more closely knit communities, given the limitations of market norms. However, following our discussion of the relationship between trust and power (and trust and control), we do not consider social capital in organizations as a substitute for either economic exchange (contracts) or authority (rules), but as a complement to management theories and practices that are preoccupied with the functioning of hierarchical and/or market relations (cf. Adler, 2001).

In order to capture the collective and relational nature of social capital, we draw on a number of complementary definitions. A good starting point is Bourdieu's seminal definition of social capital as "the aggregate of the actual or potential resources which are linked to possession of a durable network" (Bourdieu, 1986, pp. 248–249). However, we do not engage with Bourdieu's theory of how social capital is intertwined with economic and cultural capital, and we do not buy into his insistence that the outcomes of possession of social capital are reducible to economic capital and thus economic benefits (just as we do not subscribe to the tenets of rational choice theory) (Portes, 1998). Later definitions, building on Bourdieu, are arguably more helpful in capturing the collective, action-oriented and purposive workings of social capital in an organizational context. Lin (2001, pp. 24–25) provides an operational baseline definition of social capital as *resources embedded in social networks that can be accessed and used by actors to support purposive action*. Nahapiet and Ghoshal (1998) similarly define social capital as

> the sum of the actual and potential resources embedded within, available through, and derived from the network of relationships possessed by an individual or social unit. Social capital thus comprises both the network and the assets that may be mobilized through that network.
>
> (p. 243)

Adler and Kwon (2002) outline the individual and organizational implications of the concept – covering both bonding and bridging aspects:

> Through investment in building their network of external relations, both individual and collective actors can augment their social capital and thereby gain benefits in the form of superior access to information, power, and solidarity; and by investing in the development of their internal relations, collective actors can strengthen their collective identity and augment their capacity for collective action.
>
> (p. 21)

Following Szreter and Woolcock (2003, p. 6), "social capital is not a property of individuals, *per se*, it is (…) a property of their relations with each other, occupying the abstract space of relationships between individuals". These are indeed abstract formulations, but this is par for the course as they seek to maintain an understanding of social capital as, again, a collective and relational phenomenon that is not reducible to individual manifestations. A number of features of these definitions are important, not least the distinction between actual and potential resources, going back to Bourdieu, as it suggests an ongoing (perhaps unfulfilled) development potential. Social capital (like trust) is always in the making. Social capital is about having and giving access to networks of relationships and the assets that can be mobilized through such networks. It requires ongoing investment and can in turn be supportive of individual and collective action, collective identity and solidarity.

Speaking of solidarity, many definitions of social capital share an instrumental and goal-oriented focus on enabling and empowering action. However, keeping in mind contextual differences, the Danish discourse on organizational social capital has embraced a wider variety of concerns and desirable effects that have to do with social welfare and solidarity. To iterate, social capital has been framed as a matter of building strong working environments and supporting social and psychological well-being in the workplace. Ideals of community, social cohesion and inclusion are meant to strengthen the individual sense of belonging, identity and purpose, while the focus on collaboration and coordination based on trust is meant to strengthen collective action and performance, including knowledge sharing and access to information and other resources such as collegial support. Social capital is basically meant to strengthen managers' and employees' access to each other and each other's resources. In sum, the Danish discourse has explicitly addressed social capital not just as an instrumental win (relating to action), but as a win-win, benefiting the well-being of employees as well as organizational performance.

However, apart from "Social Capital" being a favored label for such win-win endeavors, the question remains: how can we capture its functioning in more granular relational terms? The upside of social capital refers to those aspects of social life – networks, norms and trust – that make it possible for social actors to work together and pursue common goals (Putnam, 1995; Leana & van Buren, 1999). Whereas economic capital is quantifiable in monetary terms, and human capital concerns the individual's knowledge and skills, social capital is fundamentally relational. The value and advantages that accrue to social capital emerge out of relationships with others. Starting from social capital, and emphasizing its collective qualities, we can consider trust as a currency that forms part of an economy. However, it is a social economy that operates on the basis of rules and exchanges that differ from those of other economies.

When you invest your time, effort and knowledge in social capital, you are investing in something that is shared and accessible to others. Social capital, as we define it here, is a *public* or *collective good* (Coleman, 1988; Leana & van Buren, 1999) to which no one has exclusive ownership rights (Burt, 1992; Nahapiet & Ghoshal, 1998). This can lead to free-rider problems if people see opportunities to gain from social capital without investing in it themselves. Ideally, however, usage of social capital – particularly of the bonding kind – is nonrivalrous in the sense that one person's use of it does not diminish its availability to others. This reflects the mechanism of the positive-sum and a sort of reversed scarcity argument: the more social capital is used, the more of it there will be. In parallel, trust can be considered as a social or moral resource that is depleted not through use, but rather through *not* being used (Gambetta, 1988; Hirschman, 1984). However, there is both an opportunity- and a risk-side to social capital. Unlike pure public goods, social capital does involve the (less ideal and very real) possibility that some people can be excluded from a given network of relations and resources (Adler & Kwon, 2002). We return to these problems of free-riding and exclusion.

A relational economy is, for better or worse, a diffuse and open economy. Whereas economic goods have a specific price, expressed in a quantitative medium of exchange, social commitments are more abstract and non-specific. This is, as Blau (1986, pp. 94–95) have argued, not just a methodological problem, it is a substantial fact. It is not only researchers who find it difficult to measure the value of social acceptance and support; social actors are also bound to experience such difficulties. The advantages of social exchange are often valued in a symbolic and intangible way that reflects underlying goodwill and reciprocity between parties. Following Adler and Kwon (2002), the use of the term *capital* should be taken somewhat metaphorically, as the efforts involved in building it (unlike, in some cases, its benefits) are not amenable to quantified measurement.

In the social dimension, obligations are diffuse in nature. What you receive or give as part of social exchange is understood as a favor or a gift, and this carries an implicit expectation of future reciprocation – although this is not precisely determined either with regard to content (what) or timing (when). If there are specific demands or use of force involved in the exchange, we are no longer talking about social relations, but about hierarchical or market relations (Portes, 1998). While social capital requires investment to flourish (Bourdieu, 1986; Dolfsma et al., 2009; Nahapiet & Ghoshal, 1998; Portes, 1998), it is investment under particular conditions and involving particular risks, which we will describe more in-depth using literature on gift exchange. It is worth mentioning that the ability to establish and make use of social relations in organizations is not entirely separate from established power structures, including the powers and mandates built into certain positions in the hierarchy (Adler & Kwon, 2002; Lee, 2009). However, the relational perspective stresses that social capital (like power) is not determined by structural and institutional factors alone. As reflected in the above definitions, social capital works through the medium of networks, and networks differ from formal organizational structures. Possession of formal managerial power (mandate) is reflective of authority but by no means synonymous with access to organizational social capital.

The open form of social exchange means that social capital and efforts to promote it transcend rule following and command and control using the force of authority. In other words, social capital cannot be managed or governed directly (Prusak & Cohen, 2001). As is the case with trust, social capital is something that managers can promote and encourage, but not force. We will now turn to the concrete matter of how organizational social capital can nevertheless be addressed explicitly and promoted in a public sector context.

Three Forms of Organizational Social Capital

Starting from the Danish experience, organizational approaches to social capital have been institutionalized under the three headings: *Bonding, Bridging* and *Linking* – based on the work of Peter Hasle and colleagues (Hasle et al., 2010). Institutionalization is here taken to mean that the framework constitutes a widely agreed-upon and taken for granted understanding of "Social Capital" among Danish organizations, public and private. Of the three headings, the first two are arguably more developed than the third (linking), which is less firmly rooted in the academic literature (see Adler & Kwon, 2002, and others who focus solely on bonding and bridging). Hasle et al.'s application of these three headings is an illustrative example of how concepts can be transferred from a societal context and put to use in organizational settings. Thus, Hasle et al. build primarily on the work of development researcher Michael Woolcock (1998), who have used these headings to outline the importance of social relations in Third World development contexts. According to Szreter and Woolcock (2003, our emphases),

> *Bonding* social capital refers to trusting and co-operative relations between members of a network who see themselves as being similar, in terms of their shared social identity. *Bridging* social capital, by contrast, comprises relations of respect and mutuality between people who know that they are not alike in some socio-demographic (or social identity) sense (differing by age, ethnic group, class, etc.). […] We would define *linking* social capital as norms of respect and networks of trusting relationships between people who are interacting across explicit, formal or institutionalized power or authority gradients in society.
>
> (pp. 5–6)

Szreter and Woolcock illustrate the value of the concept of linking social capital with reference to empirical studies, which show how

> especially in poor communities, it is the nature and extent (or lack thereof) of respectful and trusting ties to representatives of formal institutions – e.g. bankers, law enforcement officers, social workers, health care providers – that has a major bearing on their welfare.
>
> (ibid., p. 6)

To iterate, Woolcock's concepts are, first and foremost, applied to development work in socially and economically challenged communities, and – all things being equal – this is some way from the types of relationships that constitute life in modern, professional organizations in the Global North. As a case in point, Szreter (2002) writes:

> Michael Woolcock's concept of linking social capital refers to the relationships of exchange, which are established between parties who know themselves not only to be unalike, as in the case of bridging social capital, but furthermore to be unequal in their power and their access to resources, as is often the case in development work, where a range of "external" agencies interact with relatively poor societies and communities.
>
> (p. 579)

Applying this framework to the public sector in a modern liberal democracy, we encounter more homogeneity, more formal organization and more entrenched institutionalized demands and expectations serving to underpin exchanges. We can not only assume similarities and shared social identity at the level of bonding social capital. We would also expect the individual or collective actors engaged in bridging social capital to be relatively similar. That is, what divides them is not deep-seated cultural differences or inequalities, but more mundane differences related to the division of labor between different organizations and sectors, vested interests and the prevalence of different professional logics and norms. Social identities are also bound to be more fleeting and exchangeable as they are related to organizational membership rather than invariant categories such as ethnicity or social class. Although we need to account for organizational culture as a codeterminant of bridging social capital, we are still comparing professional relations and professional cultures in the context of efforts to engage in formal collaboration. Thus, we can expect a certain sameness to prevail and act as an antecedent in bridging social capital. Moreover, institutional trust plays an important role here as provider of framework conditions enabling (or failing to enable) bridging relations. Likewise, with regard to linking, we would expect the key actors to be less unalike and less unequal than in Woolcock's account. After all, managers (superiors) are often former employees (subordinates) and are to some extent subject to and part of the same organizational culture as the people they manage. And subordinates can often self-identify with the roles and tasks of their superiors.

Overall, organizational/managerial/professional uses of the Bonding-Bridging-Linking framework are bound to encounter smaller differences and a limited cultural range compared to the original use. However, we do not question its pragmatic and instrumental worth. This framework, by singling out three distinct mechanisms through which organizational social capital is brought to bear, can serve as a heuristic providing a structural backbone to our understanding of the actual and potential workings of social capital in a public sector context.

Translated into an organizational context, *Bonding* is seen to reflect circular processes, that is, efforts to create strong relationships and social cohesion within particular departments groups or subunits within an organization. *Bridging* social capital refers to horizontal and collaborative processes that transcend the boundaries of the organization (or those of a particular department, group or subunit). It is about bridge-building between different functions, silos or areas of responsibility. Moreover, this perspective harbors opportunities for co-creative relationships, partnerships and networking between public organizations and civil society (voluntary) organizations. *Linking* social capital adds a vertical perspective as it emphasizes the importance of relationships between hierarchical layers, for example, between managers and employees, and between different layers of the chain of command, ideally including the level of political decision-makers.

We consider these three forms as distinct ways of working with or addressing problems and solutions regarding social capital. They focus on different types of relationships and reflect different managerial challenges. The three forms are interconnected in different ways, but we do not presuppose any systemic relationship between them. They might be said to represent the operational (bonding), tactical (bridging) and strategic (linking) ways of working with social capital, and we will elaborate on this below. In order to further clarify the kind of relationships and processes in question, we proceed to give more extensive accounts of what they each entail.

Bonding Social Capital

Bonding social capital is concerned with the creation of strong and enduring work units and working environments. As a starting point, we are dealing with a relatively well-defined (part of an) organization with clear boundaries and a relatively well-defined scope of managerial action. It can be a public organization in its entirety, or a department, group or subunit within a larger organization. In larger organizations, bonding social capital will usually be addressed at local levels and not encompass the entire organization. Focus is on the local sense of community, the local culture and identity, the local working environment, local team-building – alongside local work relations, modes of collaboration and experiences of trust. Bonding social capital is about fostering stronger internal relationships in order to bolster employee well-being, motivation and job satisfaction, as well as productivity and perhaps creativity and innovation. Addressing matters of social capital can be a way to move the dial toward a more collaborative mindset and more reliance on trust in internal relations. This can be supported by conspicuous efforts ranging from "Social Capital" initiatives to seminars, competitions and team-building exercises, but everyday experiences of work, management, social relations, collaboration and trust are bound to be more important determinants. The ideal to strive for is an organization epitomized by mutual commitment, close cooperation and good communication, in which employees are ready to help and support each other socially and professionally. In other words, a working environment characterized by a "giving" mentality, as opposed to a purely transactional one in which it is "every man or woman for him- or herself", reflecting opportunism and action motivated solely by self-interest.

The economic argument (in a social and relational sense) is that investment in social capital helps to build a stronger organization and better conditions for organizational members to perform individually and provide support for each other's work, thus strengthening the overall, collective accomplishment and ability to perform. Apart from contributing to improved well-being and sense of belonging, investment in social capital is supposed to give better access to information, knowledge and resources and to provide, again, better opportunities for cooperation and coordination. The ideal is not necessarily an organization characterized by harmony and consensus, but rather one in which organizational members understand that they are each in a better position to do their jobs and pursue their goals if they have strong social relationships with others, and for this to work they each have to invest in this, show organizational citizenship and contribute to the creation and maintenance of social capital.

This is in many ways an organizational philosophy or mindset that assumes and requires considerable social and professional resources on the part of organizational members. People's willingness to invest in social capital is akin to their disposition to trust others. To invest in social capital normally requires a belief that the investment will be worthwhile, that it will somehow be reciprocated, appreciated or make a positive difference. Otherwise, we are in the realm of pure altruism or what von Mises (1996, p. 195) intriguingly calls *autistic exchange*: making a one-sided contribution "without the aim of being rewarded by any conduct on the part of the receiver or of third persons". We consider these orientations as outliers of social exchange. Investment in social capital will usually involve an expectation of some form of reciprocation that does not, however, have to directly benefit the investor (we expand on this in our discussion of the gift economy). Investment requires trust in the ability of the organization, the manager or colleagues to appreciate such contributions.

We can locate antecedents and barriers to development of bonding social capital at the organizational, managerial, group and individual level. At the organizational level, the question is whether or how investments in social capital are incentivized and acknowledged as having value for the organization – alongside conventional measures of individual performance. At the managerial level, it is a matter of how managers inspire investment in social capital, support relationship building among employees and appreciate team playing and team players. At the group level, it is a matter of group norms regarding collaboration and giving, while at the individual level it is a matter of, again, propensity to trust and invest in social relations.

Speaking of downsides and limitations, there are numerous social psychological obstacles that can prevent bonding social capital from flourishing, including conflicting interests, competitive rivalry, jealousy, bad chemistry, perceived injustices and differential treatment, and fallouts of conflicts between people. Given that social capital involves an investment in something that is shared and supposed to be widely accessible, there is, again, always a risk of free-riding (Adler & Kwon, 2002; Portes, 1998) – with individuals profiting from others' benevolence without making any significant investments themselves. In most cases, organizational incentive structures reward individual performance rather than contributions to "the social" and collective. Social capital may suffer due to people being too busy to invest and having a single-minded focus on their everyday work tasks and performance indicators. Other possible obstacles include high turnover of personnel, managers and/or staff, and the uncertainties and fears associated with downsizing and streamlining. After all, it makes more sense to invest in social capital if you see yourself as part of a lasting community rather than a fleeting and temporary one.

An important general critique of bonding social capital is that it lacks a more holistic and all-encompassing perspective on the organization, vis-à-vis its local focus. According to Schein (2010), organizational culture has two basic functions. One is internal integration, the other external adaptation.

Bonding social capital is exclusively preoccupied with internal integration and fails to address matters of how the organizational unit in question relates to other parts of the organization or stakeholders in the organizational environment. Local social cohesion is not an unequivocal good as such. Hence, we need to consider the insular and downward-levelling inclinations of bonding social capital. There are plenty of examples of departments or groups/enclaves/cliques/subcultures that would seem to have a high level of internal social capital among members, but are not performing well with regard to the organization's overarching goals and tend to be unreceptive and resistant to change. While internally (among the in-group) there is reciprocity, sympathy and solidarity, this fails to be the case in relationships with others (the out-group). Bonding social capital can thus be reflected in groupthink and pressures to conform to (dysfunctional) group norms. If mutual obligations become too strong, it can result in absence of critical self-reflection and development and suboptimal outcomes. We return to this theme under the heading of *othering*. Besides, bonding social capital is per definition associated with the risk of exclusion (Adler & Kwon, 2002), where some, in violation of norms of inclusion, are kept from having access to networks and resources and/or being part of the community. Reasons for such exclusion can range from differential treatment and bullying to less sinister lack of due diligence with regard to assuring inclusion of the person or persons in question.

In a public sector, where change often appears to be the only constant, and the ability and willingness to develop are much-needed properties, the bonding perspective does not suffice. It can provide a frame for well-defined, circumscribed and focused initiatives aiming to strengthen social relations and/or reduce frictions in order to support trust or reduce mistrust. However, it does not guarantee openness and proper coordination of efforts across work units. For this, we need a perspective focusing on bridge-building.

Internal and External Bridging

In practice, the bonding and bridging forms of social capital can be overlapping, as in cases where there is a need to strengthen social relations between different groups or functions within the same department or institution. However, bridging social capital really comes into its own when it transcends internal relations. That is, when we move beyond a narrow operational focus on work units and working environments and turn to tactical questions and horizontal thinking regarding relationship building between separate organizations. Bridging social capital addresses one of the major challenges in a public sector often characterized by silo thinking – namely, how can public organizations improve their ability to collaborate, coordinate their activities and create more public value in order to better serve public needs? How can more open and interdisciplinary approaches serve to reduce transaction costs and support innovation, creativity, new forms of problem-solving and user involvement? It will not happen automatically. The point that social capital requires investment becomes apparent here (Bourdieu, 1986; Nahapiet & Ghoshal, 1998; Portes, 1998; Dolfsma et al., 2009).

In public organizations, people are used to looking up rather than to the side, and collaboration with other parts of the public system is often not a high priority. This means that special efforts are called for to promote bridge-building. This is not only a matter of creating better framework conditions, including incentives for such collaboration, it is also a matter of changing mindsets and patterns of managerial action. Public managers need to be able to see the value of collaboration, to communicate it to their employees and support their acting on it. They also need to be able to communicate and collaborate with other managers across professional divisions and other boundaries. Bridging social capital is a matter of thinking in larger relational wholes, recognizing opportunities to create value together with others, instead of just focusing on predefined organizational boundaries. This in turn requires trust and a giving approach to collaboration. It requires a positive focus on opportunities to do things in ways that are smarter or better, together, rather than a negative focus on possible conflicts of interest (positive-sum instead of zero-sum). It requires horizontal communication and interaction, and thus investment of resources and energy in something more and other than the extant budget and established work tasks and ways of doing things. Among the challenges facing such development are low expectations and entrenched norms. It can be difficult to establish a sense of community and mutual obligation between organizational units whose management and employees are not accustomed to thinking and acting horizontally.

Gittell's concept of *relational coordination* has gained ground and popularity as a specialized way to handle these types of coordination problems (Gittell, 2006). The concept focuses on tasks and processes that create an urgent need for horizontal co-ordination. The three basic criteria for relational co-ordination are (1) mutual interdependence, (2) unpredictability and (3) time pressure. When these criteria are met, there is an urgent need to integrate communication and action into a larger and shared task management process. Relational coordination offers a checklist of seven points for coordination and action. They are (1) shared goals, (2) shared knowledge, (3) mutual respect, (4) problem-solving communication, (5) frequent communication, (6) timely communication and (7) accurate information (Gittell, 2006; Gittell, Godfrey & Thistlethwaite, 2012). However, Gittell's work on relational coordination and relational bureaucracy (Gittell & Douglas, 2012) has a more operational edge than what we are developing here. Where relational coordination focuses on specific tasks involving the need for collaboration and offers a technical/instrumental arsenal of tools with which to handle such challenges, we want to emphasize that bridging and coordination not only in special cases but also more generally have value and importance in relation to the quality of management and governance in and around public organizations.

As previously mentioned, New Public Governance (NPG) supports efforts to create relational organizations (see Chapter 2). NPG transcends internal relations, as it also focuses on relationships with citizens (in various roles), civil society organizations and other external stakeholders. By focusing on partnerships, co-creation and user involvement in the delivery of public services, bridging social capital serves to promote thinking in terms of networks and forging stronger relationships with the outside world (see Chapter 5). The bridge-building perspective provides an open and dynamic principle for collaboration and innovation in a public sector with constantly shifting boundaries. Bridging social capital helps to support our understanding of what it takes – and how investments can be made – to make partnerships and co-creation deliver results in practice.

Linking as Vertical Coordination

Bonding and bridging social capital are both important for the functioning of public organizations. The third form focuses on how social capital functions vertically – between hierarchical layers. This form of social capital tends to get less attention than the other two, one possible explanation is that it is closely intertwined with and perhaps difficult to disentangle from the authority relations of hierarchy. The positive theoretical or managerial argument is that there is (or ought to be) more to vertical relationships than formal authority and power mandates, and that this something "extra" can be described in terms of social capital. However, there is both an opportunity and a risk side to this argument. Szreter and Woolcock (2003) speak of how the three forms of social capital apart from their happy uses can also be put to unhappy uses, including nepotism, corruption and suppression. These are certainly very pertinent concerns with regard to linking social capital in an organizational context. On the one hand, the very idea of linking social capital would seem to fly in the face of classical bureaucratic virtues regarding division of labor and authority – and aversion to corruptible social relationships. On the other, it may point to limitations and deficiencies of the classical model and show how social relations can make a positive difference for management and governance. The notion of linking social capital can be (and is) used more or less synonymously with visible and present management and efforts to strengthen relations between hierarchical layers (e.g., heads of departments and office managers). To capture this with a little more precision (considering that linking in itself is a rather bland and generic term), we use the heading *Linking as Vertical Coordination*. This points more directly to the concrete problem and managerial challenges at hand.

Vertical relations in the public sector often tend to be characterized by loose couplings, as far as social capital goes. That is, a lack of contact, interaction and communication between those who make decisions and those who are supposed to carry them out and live with the consequences on a daily basis. This is not least reflected in strategic planning and implementation of new strategies and reforms (see Chapter 6). In organizations subject to political control, politicians and leadership can make far-reaching decisions without the approval of those directly affected, due to the parliamentary chain of command and managerial authority. The general problem is that when significant and far-reaching decisions are made in the public sector, there is often a lack of coordination between the perceptions of reality of those who make the decisions and the perceptions of reality of those who are affected by those decisions or responsible for their implementation. In many cases, this lack of coordination is caused by lack of trust, if not out-right distrust, and it can lead to bad, harmful or suboptimal decisions – both with regard to operational implications and perceptions of meaning(lessness) among those affected. This can, in turn, create noise and friction and have long-lasting negative effects on motivation, job satisfaction and the quality of the work that is carried out.

Linking as vertical coordination is about counteracting tendencies toward loose coupling or short-circuits between different layers of management and command, especially with regard to major strategic decisions. That is why we find it appropriate to describe this kind of social capital as strategic. Importantly, this is not a matter of questioning manager's right to manage and make decisions. What matters is managers' ability, willingness and courage to qualify and coordinate their decisions – and perceptions of reality – by actively involving, engaging and listening to the (middle) managers and employees on the receiving end and closer to practice. Ideally, this will lead to better decisions, better implementation and better processes. What is at stake here is managers' willingness to accept vulnerability in relations with those lower in the pecking order (as discussed in Chapter 2). That is, willingness to expose him- or herself to being corrected, contradicted or having man-agerial decisions and actions – past, present or future – challenged – through dialogue and exchange of ideas. Of course, there is a limit to this argument as there is no guarantee that any agreement or consensus can be reached. However, the important premise sustaining this argument is that resistance to managerial decisions and change is not necessarily rooted in professional conservatism, contrarian efforts to protect existing privileges and the like – it can also stem from qualified and matter of fact assessments that the decisions (relating to reforms, strategies, etc.) with which managers and workers must contend, do not seem meaningful or provide optimal support for the work that needs to be done.

The notion of linking as vertical coordination suggests that public man-agers and decision-makers should have the courage and willingness to make contact with lower levels of the hierarchy. It is imperative that they occa-sionally leave their offices and take the time to invest in social relations in order to inform, qualify and, in the final analysis, strengthen the basis on which they make and implement their decisions. In organizations subject to political control, even the most senior managers are required to imple-ment decisions that they would rather have been without and which would not have been made had it been up to them. It is important that managers are able to act as a form of buffer and that they are to some degree able to absorb or mitigate the negative effects of such decisions. They will be better able to do this if they have quick access to information about a decision's unfavorable consequences in order to determine how the situation might be improved. This in turn requires social capital. At the same time, the need for vertical coordination also highlights the importance of middle managers being able, to some extent, "lead up" and influence decision making by more senior management when the situation calls for it. This, too, requires investment in social capital.

In sum, these are the three basic ways of working with social capital in and around public organizations. More can be said about them and more will be said in Chapter 5, where we go through a number of empirical examples of how the trust and social capital agendas have been put into action. However, before moving onto our discussion of the gift economy and how it relates to bonding, bridging and linking, we need to take a step back and address the issue of difference. As we have argued, organizational and professional translations of social capital tend to assume a certain sameness among social actors and to operate within a rather limited cultural range. Next, we turn to resulting problems and solutions in the realms of *diversity* and *othering*.

Social Capital, Diversity and the Problem of Othering

While diversity is a significant blind spot in the literature on organizational social capital, the notion of othering provides us with not only a vantage point for reflecting on diversity issues, but also a way to address divisive tendencies in modern organizations more generally. Divisive tendencies that social capital and relational thinking can help to address and, perhaps, ameliorate.

While the literature on organizational social capital, as we have seen, puts emphasis on consensus and value congruence (Adler & Kwon, 2002; Leana & van Buren, 1999), the critical diversity literature is better suited to address matters of conflict and power relations, including issues of inequality. At the organizational level, social capital has become synonymous with efforts to create a strong sense of community and collaboration based on shared values and goals. Adler, Heckscher and Prusak (2011, p. 96) speak of how "collaborative communities seek a basis for trust and organizational cohesion that is more robust than self-interest, more flexible than tradition, and less ephemeral" than the emotional appeal of charismatic leaders. However, as Mor Barak et al. (2016) point out in regard to diversity management and its prospects of fostering a climate for inclusion: If, and only if, organizational members feel included and perceive that they are part of the same group or team will there be basis for a sense of community and shared interest to develop among them.

Research contributions under the headings of trust and social capital in management and organization studies arguably fail to address more deep-seated issues regarding inequality, inclusion/exclusion and power asymmetries. They fail to take account of, for instance, how "most members of minority groups do not feel a sense of belonging to the organizations they are part of because of the persistent fixation on them as being different" (Ghorashi & Sabelis, 2013, p. 82). They tend to assume value congruence (or at least the possibility hereof) among relatively homogeneous and like-minded individuals. And they tend to foreground consensus-based ideals of social organization rather than the tensions and conflicts that are bound to be involved in efforts to reach those ideals. Therefore (and this book is no different), it comes across as somewhat generic and idealized in addressing issues of diversity and defining what it takes to create more equal organizations or processes to that effect.

To speak of othering is one way to address problems of diversity and organizational difference and divisiveness more generally. While notions of the other, otherness and othering are front and center in the diversity debate, they are largely absent from the literature on organizational social capital. As we have seen, loosely based on the Danish trajectory, there is a tendency for "the other" to be quite similar in this literature, regardless of whether we are talking about bonding, bridging or linking social capital. In other words, it is assumed, if only implicitly, that the differences between the involved parties have more to do with organizational membership and professional allegiances than more deep-seated cultural differences. The concept of othering is able to capture both types of differences.

Othering can be defined as a "process of casting a group, an individual or an object into the role of the 'other' and establishing one's own identity through opposition to and, frequently, vilification of this Other" (Gabriel, 2012). In society, problems of othering are perhaps most clearly expressed in relation to differences regarding race, ethnicity, gender, religion and sexual identity. However, modern organizations not only mirror the forms of othering that dominate public discourse, they also contain their own more mundane forms related to hierarchy, market mechanisms (competitive relations in the organization), group formation, and professional and physical divisions and silos.

Othering involves relegation of the other to a lower status and is reflective of disdain, disapproval, lack of respect or recognition. It comes to the fore in willful or ingrained (taken for granted) value judgments that make use of particular identity markers to create and maintain social distance and divisiveness among individuals or groups, often based on ignorance. It is reflected in all kinds of communication that expresses a negative or reductive view of others based on a single identity marker. Elements of othering are built into language, and othering is most easily identifiable in language use and communicative representation of others. By means of othering, a heterogeneous group can be made homogeneous and be reduced to a stereotype without nuance and individuality – while highlighting differences between "us" and "them".

However, as Foucault have reminded us, power is relational and multi-directional. Othering is therefore not a one-way street. It does not suffice to consider othering as an act of (powerful) perpetrators upon (powerless) victims (of oppression, discrimination, etc.). Instead of docile (othered, objectified) bodies, we assume the existence of human subjects capable of acting against the processes of othering they encounter – and capable of engaging in their own modes of othering. For example, management's othering of employees can (and will often) result in employees' othering of management in a mutually reinforcing (negative) process or spiral.

NPM is an illustrative example of how othering can work both ways. Hence, NPM can be described as a technology – and a mindset – with othering properties, due to its underlying negative assumptions about human behavior. Managerial uses of NPM can lead to an othering of frontline personnel as either opportunistic knaves who do as little as they can get away with, or idealistic knights, who cannot manage budgets, are immune to economic reasoning and lack a sense of the bigger picture (see Chapter 3). Conversely, employee experiences with the use of such tools can lead to othering of managers as bureaucrats with cold hands that are only or primarily concerned with budgets, economic savings and spreadsheets. For managers, othering can serve to justify monitoring and control, and thus restriction of employee freedom and autonomy. On the part of employees, othering can serve to justify that management decrees are either ignored or pushed aside as meaningless or counter-productive. Moreover, public managers can be othered as political animals motivated by their careers rather than what is best for the organization – thus lacking a deeper sense of commitment and purpose. This can also serve to justify direct or indirect opposition and resistance to management decisions.

Othering is imbued with a particular duality. On the one hand, it can be supportive of management decisions and the exercise of power and control. On the other, it can undermine the basis for decisions to have the desired effects. Why consult with employees if they tend to work against management and are immune to rational arguments? Why follow managers if they have their heads in the clouds and are out of touch with practical realities on the ground? This process can, as previously mentioned, be mutually self-reinforcing. If management and governance initiatives do not produce the desired results, it can serve as an affirmation both of management's othering of employees and employee's othering of management (vis-à-vis the tendency for distrust to be self-affirming). This can result in management becoming more controlling, which in turn can trigger a stronger backlash and more alienation among employees.

Othering removes nuances and instead offers a binary code useful for reducing complexity, confirming prejudices and attributing blame to others – often based on the belief that "the problem is with them – they're in the wrong, not us". Othering is thus a way of denying other people or groups of people reason, dignity and individual recognition. It is arguably an everyday occurrence in modern organizations – between managers and employees, between professions and professional groups and so on. Importantly, othering tends to thrive in relations characterized by lack of knowledge, lack of personal experience and lack of direct contact (with the other(s)). Othering can, in a negative or dysfunctional way, be integral to social identity and social integration at group level in organizations (vis-à-vis the downward-levelling norms of bonding social capital). You become an integrated part of the group by taking part in, confirming and conforming to an "us" vs. "them" narrative denigrating other people or other groups and serving to create or maintain distance.

It is easier to look down on others and reduce them to stereotypes if you have limited knowledge about them or limited contact with them. This is where social capital comes in. The work on strengthening social relations is basically about counteracting othering, separation and fragmentation. Hence, occurrences of othering are bound to make not only bridging and linking, but also bonding (vis-à-vis the diversity issue) more difficult. It is about challenging prejudices and the lazy comfort of old habits ("This is how things are here; this is how we have always done things; this is how we have always seen ourselves in relation to others"). Othering is impossible when a group identifies with another group, and social capital is very much a matter of supporting mutual identification and better understanding of each other across and throughout the organization. As already mentioned, the language used is important. Are others referred to as part of a common "we" or in terms of "us" and "them"? Is the language used serving to unite rather than divide? Distance – both physical and mental – can be an obstacle to such efforts. Physical distance may seem like a trivial problem, but we should not underestimate the importance of the physical environment – not only for how work is carried out, but also for how it enables (or disables) people from different units to meet, interact and "bump into each other" occasionally. Psychological distance can to some extent be shortened by creating opportunities for people from different parts of the organization to meet and by ensuring that as much work as possible involves physical presence (as opposed to virtual participation).

These considerations also apply to managers in relation to employees and to senior management in relation to middle managers. This brings us back to the definition of trust as a risk-filled choice, a leap of faith that involves acceptance of vulnerability (see Chapter 2). While othering tends to provide an affirmation of the need to make use of repressive powers, trust-based leadership is very much about breaking down the barriers and forms of partition, that othering is a reflection of, through more openness, forthcomingness and more equal relations. The other, or others, will often seem less foolish or incompetent, and perhaps even sensible, once you take the time to sit down and talk to them in person. Again, the ideal here is not some rarefied form of harmony and consensus, but rather understanding and fundamental recognition of the (otherness of the) other.

The Gift Economy

As our final order of business in this chapter we turn to notions of gift-giving and gift economy as a way to crystalize and bring to the fore fundamentals of social capital and trust-based leadership. The notion of recognition provides an obvious segue. To give recognition to another (e.g., to a colleague for an extraordinary effort, a job well done or in appreciation of a particular action or behavior) can be seen as a favor and thus a gift, and as such it forms part of the social economy of an organization.

We contend that thinking about social relations in organizations as gift relations and of the organization as a form of gift economy is one way to make actual and potential benefits of trust and social capital more tangible. The argument arguably sounds more radical than it is. Gift exchange is the quintessential form of social exchange (Boulding, 1981), and it plays a vital role in the construction of all sorts of networks and forms of collaboration (Dolfsma et al., 2009). Following Portes (1998, p. 5), "Resources obtained through social capital have, from the point of view of the recipient, the character of a gift". Adloff (2021, p. 15) suggests that "without gifts, no society can exist". Whether or how the same argument applies to organizations is of course debatable. We will argue that it does apply, in the sense that most organizations would rapidly collapse if their managers and employees stopped giving more to each other (in the form of mutual help and support) than they are formally obliged to give. We would expect to find elements of gift economy in virtually all organizations. Whether this is seen as a positive or as a reflection of how organizations are able to exploit collegial loyalty is another matter (cf. Adloff, 2021).

Either way, the giving nature or qualities of organizational relations are often not recognized – either in theory or practice. Adloff (2021) argues that

> almost all social theories have woefully neglected this dimension of human activity. Gifts are either ignored or explained away. Typically, gifts are accounted for in two ways: either they are reduced to the fact that people do what norms expect of them; or they are attributed to motives of self-interest. However, there is a human tendency to the gift that cannot be explained in a normativistic and utilitarian manner – gifts embody moments of surplus and unconditionality, which are constitutive for the creation of sociality. Thus, at the base of the social (…) are non-equivalences and asymmetries, because giving is not reducible to the exchange of equivalent values.
>
> (p. 15)

Baviera, English and Guillén (2016, p. 159) similarly argue that scholarship in the realms of "management, economic analysis, and organizational behaviour have tended to neglect or marginalize the phenomenon of giving". Thus, apart from specialized treatments in the social capital, social exchange and gift economy literatures, there is a tendency to neglect the giving nature of human and social relationships. While we concur with Adloff with regard to non-equivalence and asymmetry in gift relations, and how such relations are not reducible to a utilitarian (market) logic and self-interest, we do not find unconditionality to be the best way to describe the functioning of gift exchange. Baviera et al. (2016) similarly want to explain the social phenomenon of "giving for nothing", and thus how unconditional, interpersonal giving of time and resources come about. They argue that such generosity is widespread and is crucial to the success of many organizations. While we concur with the latter points, we argue that giving tends to be "for something" and is indeed conditional (vis-à-vis the relational understanding of trust) – and that it is the conditionality of gift-giving that makes it interesting to discuss as a relational practice in organizations. The notion of "giving for nothing" is arguably more reflective of the moral trust paradigm.

However, there are perhaps good reasons for the neglect of the gift in the context of management and organization. Are the conditions for gift exchange not undermined by the prevalence of hierarchy (asymmetrical power relations) and market (competitive relations and economic exchange)? You may ask: Is it possible to give gifts in organizations? Our immediate answer is: It happens all the time, and it happens through social exchange. Turning to Adloff (2021) once more, he explicitly addresses the problem of how gift exchange applies to organizations. Although organizational relationships are to some extent impersonal relationships, he argues, this does not exclude the possibility that the logic of the gift can be brought to bear. In the shadow of formal structures and exchanges (hierarchy and market), "informal relationships always emerge in organisations, which are based on the logic of the gift, and without which the organisation could not survive" (p. 19). He concludes that no organization can manage without the commitment of organizational members to give something to colleagues or the whole organization.

The same point applies to gift exchange that applies to social capital. The gift economy exists alongside hierarchical and market relations and serves to mitigate their weaknesses and limitations (Graycar & Jancsics, 2016). Whereas economic exchange is formal and often contracted explicitly (as advocated by agency theory), social exchange highlights dynamic and interactional aspects of exchange processes, including their development over time and their dependence on trust (Whitener et al., 1998). Blau (1986) argues that the basic and most crucial difference between economic exchange and social exchange is that the latter entails *unspecified* obligations: "Social exchange (…) involves the principle that one person does another a favour, and while there is a general expectation of some future return, its exact nature is definitely not stipulated in advance" (Blau, 1986, p. 93).

How to conceive of the gift, then? According to Dolfsma (2021), there are two fundamental understandings at play. The *pure* or strict understanding suggests that a gift consists in the transfer of a symbolic good without any expectation of a reciprocal action. This is the "no strings attached" view, which finds support in legal theory and practice – according to which, again, a gift does not involve any (formal) obligations on the part of the recipient. The pure understanding leads to the question of whether gift-giving can be a truly unselfish act, or whether there is always some element of self-interest involved (cf. Champetier, 2001; Derrida, 1995). This can in turn lead to a dichotomous view of, on the one hand, gifts as motivated by altruism and, on the other, exchanges motivated by self-interest as taking place in the market (Dolfsma, 2021).

The *mixed* view is our preferred view and the one that aligns with our relational take on trust and social capital. It takes its cue from classical anthropologists like Mauss and Malinowski, who have argued that gift exchange in many cases is motivated by a combination of altruism and self-interest (Dolfsma et al., 2009; Eckstein, 2001; Faldetta, 2012; Komter, 2007). The two views are antagonistic and not easy to reconcile. What causes suspicion in the pure view serves as a basic assumption in the mixed view, namely that engagement in all kinds of exchanges, including gifts, can be instigated by multiple motives. Thus, the distinction between gift and market exchange is less categorical in this view (Dolfsma, 2021). To iterate, gifts can involve mixed motives and be exchanged for purely altruistic as well as more strategic and instrumental reasons (Dolfsma et al., 2009).

Gift-giving in organizations is a prime example of this. Generally speaking, from a managerial point of view, gift exchange is not an end in itself, but a means of achieving benefits that can be described in terms of social capital. In other words, it is an investment in social relations. This underlying instrumentalism may, of course, give rise to cynicism. Does this mean that gift giving is little more than a form of enforced reciprocity – a way to manipulate employees in order to make them contribute more and accept ever more demanding requirements imposed upon them by the organization (vis-à-vis our critical discussion of post-bureaucratic organization and boundarylessness in Chapter 3)? While this certainly *can* be the case empirically (see below), it is important to emphasize that gift-giving as a management philosophy or principle has limited scope for coercion and/or manipulation, because the form, content and timing of the reciprocal action remains undetermined.

The mixed view is built on the sociological and anthropological insight that gift exchange can serve to initiate and maintain relationships between individuals, groups or organizations – and does so in a way that is particular to this form of exchange. When a gift is exchanged, it creates the expectation of a reciprocal action, a return- or counter-gift from the recipient. However, a gift does not involve expectations of an equivalent or formal return, and the value of the gift is usually left unspecified. Gifts are meant to be appreciated but not priced, and in that sense they can be characterized as "silent" (Bourdieu, 1977; Dolfsma et al., 2009). In the words of Skågeby (2010, p. 171), "The rules of gift-giving are both socialized and tacit. As such, they make up a form of practical knowledge (of which most people are aware) that has a strong potential to shape social relationships". Gifts create social bonds, but not in the form of formal obligations or requirements. In the words of Malinowski (quoted in Blau, 1986, p. 93), "the equivalence of the counter-gift is left to the giver, and it cannot be enforced by any kind of coercion". If there are specific requirements, a specific price or a definite timeframe tied to the return, we are talking about a transactional market exchange – or a case of bribery (cf. Graycar & Jancsics, 2016). Gifts are characterized by flexibility and indetermination and can therefore not be reduced to mechanical laws, closed systems or universal definitions (Komter, 2007).

It is thus a hallmark of the gift economy that you receive something other than what you give and that what you get in return is always uncertain. Thus, the return-gift has to consist of something that is different from the original gift. It is even prohibited to make an equal return "payment" in gift exchange as this is tantamount to returning the offered gift and discontinuing the relationship. Besides, the return-gift cannot be given right away. It must be deferred and occur at some later point in time for the logic of the gift to be respected (Dolfsma et al., 2009). If you give something back immediately, this is equivalent to refusing to enter into a relationship with the giver, it may even be taken as an insult. The gift and the return-gift must be separated by an unspecified time interval.

This open-endedness in terms of the nature, value and moment of the return-gift, means that gift exchange is always unbalanced. Following Belk (1979), the tensions generated in perpetually unbalanced exchanges serve as an important dynamic in gift exchange. By contrast, economic exchange involves tit-for-tat transactions and once such transactions are completed the parties can in principle start over again with a blank slate. Gift exchange involves "social debts" that are *not* resolved and which connect individual and collective actors to each other. Gifts thus serve to create bonds of goodwill and social indebtedness among people (Belk & Coon, 1993; Dolfsma et al., 2009). Coleman (1988, 1990) refers to such outstanding obligations as "credit slips" between givers and receivers. Thus, the quality we want to highlight above all about gift-giving is that it generates and supports social relations, mutual obligations and reciprocity and does so in open, dynamic and flexible ways.

Following Mauss (2000), membership of a community implies three obligations. You must be prepared to (1) give, (2) receive and (3) reciprocate. When you receive, you are obliged to give something back – you *owe*. Applied to modern organizations, this implies that members are included in the community and create and get access to social capital through acts of giving, receiving and reciprocating. Following the positive-sum argument, those who give more in a gift economy also tend to receive more, and being perceived as a creditor may increase one's status compared to being a debtor (Dolfsma et al., 2009). The same problems of inclusion and exclusion that applies to social capital applies to this argument. We address these problems as part of this chapter's final section on the managerial aspects of gift-giving.

Management as Gift-Giving

In the words of Dolfsma et al. (2009, p. 320), "Virtually any *resource* – material or immaterial, tangible or intangible, of high or low value – can be transformed into a gift or favour". It follows that, within organizations, gifts can take many forms and be given in many different ways – often implicitly (or silently). As per the distinction between hierarchy, market and social relations, it must be emphasized that gift-giving belongs to the social realm and thus to the social economy within the organization. Gifts do not belong in the same category as exchanges that are clearly determinable in terms of price or based on rights and entitlements – for example, wages, allowances and bonuses. To discuss gifts in such terms tends to muddy the waters. Gift-giving is something that takes place in social relationships between managers and employees, as well as in manager-manager relationships and collegial employee-employee relations. Furthermore, vis-à-vis internal and external bridging, it can apply to relations between different departments, groups or subunits or separate organizations. Over the years, we have had many discussions with master students about what does and what does not constitute a gift from a managerial point of view. To do a colleague a favor is the very epitome of the gift economy. However, in many cases it can be difficult to clearly and unambiguously define what a gift is or can be. Often, it matters more *how* something is given (and how it is received) than *what* is given.

From the perspective of gift exchange, management is necessarily and unavoidably about giving, and everything that goes into social exchange can be considered part of the gift economy. Examples include *assignments, resources, recognition, time, attention, presence, goodwill, feedback* (praise and criticism), *advice, guidance, support, inspiration, work flexibility* (spatial and temporal), *freedom, autonomy* and opportunities for *education and upskilling. Feedback, sparring, information, ideas* and *inspiration* are examples of gifts from employees to managers. Even *complaints* can be seen as gifts if the complainer observes a certain decorum and the timing is right. Recognition is, alongside other prosocial organizational behaviors (Brief & Motowidlo, 1986), an example of something essential that managers can give to employees (and vice versa). Luthans (2000, p. 33) speaks of "the importance of providing employees with non-financial rewards such as recognition and attention" and how this "type of reward can be very effective and efficient because it doesn't cost anything, is available for everyone to use, and no one gets too much of it". In the words of Moss Kanter (quoted in Luthans, 2000, p. 33), "Recognition is so easy to do and so inexpensive to distribute that there is simply no excuse for not doing it".

Importantly, recognition is not given automatically, nor is it communicated automatically – although judging by their actions some managers seem to think it is. The gift economy calls for investment and risk taking. One essential quality of the focus on gift exchange is that it calls attention to little things, small efforts that can be of great value and make a big difference. As a manager, or colleague, are you good at giving, or are you too stingy? Are you generous at all? Or perhaps too generous. Do you deploy your generosity wisely? Do you invest enough in social capital? In the hustle and bustle of everyday work life, do you take time out and make an effort to acknowledge a job well done or give colleagues attention and feedback? What we are advocating is not positive psychology in the form of, for example, *appreciative inquiry*. If positive feedback becomes a rule-like requirement or expectation, it becomes meaningless at best – although deserved praise can, of course, be a gift. However, the gift economy idea is at odds with managers who see no reason to give praise or acknowledge employees who are doing the work they are supposed to do and paid to do, and mainly provide negative feedback when mistakes are made. If doing a good job is the norm and what is expected of people, why reward them for it? From the perspective of the gift economy, the answer is that it is an investment in social capital that ideally serves to strengthen social relations and social cohesion and commitment.

However, gift exchange, like social capital, is not without its problems and caveats. As previously mentioned, we have had many discussions with students about what constitutes a good and appropriate gift and the difficulties of maneuvering in this space. What qualifies as a good gift is usually specific to the situation, and it can to some extent – in a manager-employee relation – be specific to the person in question and his or her personality and disposition. When an employee does a good job or makes an extraordinary effort, it may not be obvious how this can best be rewarded. To be a good gift-giver often requires instinct and feel for the situation: "what kind of person am I dealing with here, and what are his or her preferences with regard to recognition, how it is given, and whether or how it is communicated to others?"

Indeed, the experience of others is more than a trivial issue here. Gift-giving in organizations tend to transcend dyadic relations. If one employee gets a gift of a certain stature, others will usually come to know this and may react negatively if they experience that a colleague's performance or achievement is singled out for praise or reward at their (perceived) detriment. We have heard quite a few accounts of such experiences – and how the reactions and possible misgivings of others have to be considered when giving gifts. However, while social capital and gift-giving are inclusive ideas, they are not egalitarian. There will never be an equal distribution of social capital and gifts in organizations. The gift economy is not about everyone having or being entitled to the same amount of resources. The ideal is equality in terms of access and opportunity, not in terms of equal outcomes. As a result, the positive, relationship building effects of gift exchange will face ongoing challenges related to favoritism, differential treatment, perceived injustices and discrimination. With regard to the latter, does the organizational gift economy provide a level playing field for all members to give, receive and reciprocate?

Part of the mundane managerial challenge is to avoid gift-giving that while positive and motivating to some (the recipients) causes dissatisfaction and demotivation elsewhere in the organization. Or rather, it is about creating a positive-sum mindset according to which such giving is not frowned upon, but rather seen as a positive reflection of recognition that many can share in and feel part of as colleagues. Speaking of access and entitlement, however, there are also "gift wishes" that cannot be honored because they are not considered a good investment at a particular moment in time. Examples of this include employees asking for particular assignments or making requests with regard to education and upskilling. There can be a huge gap between what employees feel they deserve or are entitled to and what managers consider to be worth investing in. Some employees can be almost impossible to satisfy. It applies to managers and employees at all levels – they can be good or bad at giving, receiving and reciprocating. Moreover, a gift economy can be both including and excluding. This has partly to do with the deferred nature of the return-gift. The time interval between receiving a gift and responding in kind is a constitutive part of the gift relationship, but there are limits to how long the interval can be drawn out if you wish to remain part of the organization. If you receive and receive but show no ability or willingness to give anything back, trust is bound to wear thin and you risk being excluded (fired or let go).

Although gift exchange is often about personal relationships, it transcends dyadic manager-employee, manager-manager or employee-employee relations. It also applies to the organizational level, allowing us to talk about the organization as a gift economy or a gift system (akin to speaking of trust culture). Using concepts from the literature on social exchange, it is about creating a basis not only for *restricted exchange* between A (manager) and B (employee), but also for *generalized exchange*, where A gives to B, who gives to C (who may be another employee) (Ekeh, 1974, pp. 47–49). Dolfsma et al. (2009) make the distinction between an indirect and a community form of generalized exchange, where the community form highlights the multi-party nature of social exchange and norms of reciprocity. In the words of Ekeh (1974, p. 59), communities characterized by norms of generalized exchange "enjoy a *credit mentality*: the belief that individuals are credit worthy and can be trusted to pay back what they owe".

This highlights the importance of fostering a giving mindset among managers and employees and of establishing a giving culture in the organization. Importantly, this is not just a matter of bonding social capital. The giving mindset can also extend to internal and external bridging and be an important antecedent for development in the realm of collaboration, co-creation and partnerships between separate public organizations and other actors (Thygesen & Löfvall, 2020). In sum, we can say that gift exchange is significant for the development of bonding social capital and internal and external bridging in particular. It is about creating organizational units characterized by a giving mentality and counteracting division and othering. In giving organizations, managers and employees have access to more resources and this is supportive of better performance. A giving mentality is also important for efforts to promote interdisciplinary collaboration and external partnerships and networking. Next, in Chapter 5, we provide a treatment and discussion of how the trust agenda and social capital have been enacted in practice in the public sector.

References

Adler, P. S. (2001). Market, hierarchy, and trust: The knowledge economy and the future of capitalism. *Organization Science*, 12(2), 215–234.

Adler, P. S., Heckscher, C. & Prusak, L. (2011). Building a collaborative enterprise. *Harvard Business Review*, July–August, 95–101.

Adler, P. S. & Kwon, S.-W. (2002). Social capital: Prospects for a new concept. *Academy of Management Review*, 27(1), 17–40.

Adler, P. S., Kwon, S. & Heckscher, C. (2008). Professional work: The emergence of collaborative community. *Organization Science*, 19, 359–376.

Adloff, F. (2021). Institutional orders and the gift: A macrosociological approach. In Kesting, S., Negru, I. & Silvestri, P. (Eds.). *The gift in the economy and society. Perspectives from institutional economics and other social sciences* (15–33). London: Routledge.

Ariely, D. (2008). *Predictably irrational*. St. Ives: Harper.

Baker, W. B. & Faulkner, R. R. (2009). Social capital, double embeddedness, and mechanisms of stability and change. *American Behavioral Scientist*, 52, 1531–1555.

Baviera, T., English, W. & Guillén, M. (2016). The "logic of gift": Inspiring behavior in organizations beyond the limits of duty and exchange. *Business Ethics Quarterly*, 26(2), 159–180.

Belk, R. W. (1979). Gift-giving behavior. In J. Sheth (Ed.). *Research in marketing, vol. 2*. Greenwich, CT: JAI Press.

Belk, R. W. & Coon, G. S. (1993). Gift giving as agapic love: An alternative to the exchange paradigm based on dating experiences. *The Journal of Consumer Research*, 20, 393–417.

Blau, P. M. (1986). *Exchange & power in social life*. New Brunswick, NJ: Transaction Publishers.

Boulding, K. (1981). *A preface to grant economics – The economics of love and fear*. Cambridge: Cambridge University Press.

Bourdieu, P. (1977). *Outline of a theory of practice*. Cambridge: Cambridge University Press.

Bourdieu, P. (1986). Forms of capital. In J. G. Richardson (Ed.). *Handbook of theory and research for the sociology of education* (241–258). New York: Greenwood Press.

Brief, A. P. & Motowidlo, S. J. (1986). Prosocial organizational behaviors. *The Academy of Management Review*, 11(4), 710–725.

Burt, R. S. (1992). *Structural holes: The social structure of competition*. Cambridge, MA: Harvard University Press.

Champetier, C. (2001). The philosophy of the gift: Jacques Derrida, Martin Heidegger. *Angelaki. Journal of the Theoretical Humanities*, 6(2), 15–22.

Coleman, J. S. (1988). Social capital: In the creation of human capital. *American Journal of Sociology*, 94 (Supplement), 95–120.

Coleman, J. S. (1990). *The foundations of social theory*. Cambridge, Mass: Harvard University Press.

Derrida, J. (1995). *The gift of death*. Chicago: University of Chicago Press.

Dolfsma, W. (2021). Afterword. The puzzle of the gift. In Kesting, S., Negru, I. & Silvestri, P. (Eds.). *The gift in the economy and society. Perspectives from institutional economics and other social sciences* (203–209). London: Routledge.

Dolfsma, W., van der Eijk, R. & Jolink, A. (2009). On a source of social capital: Gift exchange. *Journal of Business Ethics*, 89, 315–329.

Eckstein, S. (2001). Community as gift-giving: Collective roots of volunteerism. *American Sociological review*, 66(6), 829–851.

Ekeh, P. (1974). *Social exchange theory: The two traditions.* Cambridge, Mass: Harvard University Press.

Faldetta, G. (2012). The logic of gift and gratuitousness in business relationships. *Journal of Business Ethics,* 100, 67–77.

Gabriel,Y. (2012). *The other and othering – A short introduction.* Downloaded from: www. yiannisgabriel.com

Gambetta, D. (1988). Can we trust trust? In D. Gambetta (Ed.) (1988). *Trust: Making and breaking cooperative relations* (213–237). Oxford: Blackwell.

Ghorashi, H. & Sabelis, I. (2013). Juggling difference and sameness: Rethinking strategies for diversity in organizations. *Scandinavian Journal of Management,* 29, 78–86.

Gittell, J. H. (2006). Relational coordination: Coordinating work through relationships of shared goals, shared knowledge and mutual respect. In O. Kyriakidou & M. Ozbilgin (Eds.). *Relational perspectives in organizational studies: A research companion* (74–94). Northampton, MA: Edward Elgar.

Gittell, J. H. & Douglass, A. (2012). Relational bureaucracy: Structuring reciprocal relationships into roles. *The Academy of Management Review,* 37(4), 709–733.

Gittell, J. H., Godfrey, M. & Thistlethwaite, J. (2012). Editorial. Interprofessional collaborative practice and relational coordination: Improving healthcare through relationships. *Journal of Interprofessional Care,* Early Online: 1–4. DOI: 10.3109/13561820.2012.730564

Graycar, A. & Jancsics, D. (2016). Gift giving and corruption. *International Journal of Public Administration,* 40(12), 1013–1023.

Hasle, P., Thoft, E. & Olesen, K. G. (2010). *Ledelse med social capital,* Latvia: L&R Business.

Hirschman, A. O. (1984). Against parsimony: Three easy ways of complicating some categories of economic discourse. *American Economic Review Proceedings,* 74, 88–96.

Klijn, E. H. & Koppenjan, J. (2016). *Governance networks in the public sector.* Oxon: Routledge.

Komter, A. (2007). Gifts and social relations: The mechanisms of reciprocity. *International Sociology,* 22(1), 93–107.

Kwon, S.-W. & Adler, P. S. (2014). Social capital: Maturation of a field of research. *Academy of Management Review,* 39(4), 412–422.

Leana, C. R. & van Buren, H. J. (1999). Organizational social capital and employment practices. *Academy of Management Review,* 24(3), 538–555.

Lee, R. (2009). Social capital and business and management: Setting a research agenda. *International Journal of Management Reviews,* 11(3), 247–273.

Lin, N. (2001). *Social capital. A theory of social structure and action.* Milton Keynes: Cambridge University Press.

Luthans, K. (2000). Recognition: A powerful, but often overlooked, leadership tool to improve employee performance. *The Journal of Leadership Studies,* 7(1), 31–39.

Mauss, M. (2000). *The gift: Forms and functions of exchange in archaic societies.* New York: Norton.

von Mises, L. (1996). *Human action – A treatise on economics.* San Francisco: Fox & Wilkes.

Mor Barak, M. E., Lizano, E. L., Kim, A., Duan, L., Rhee, M.-K., Hsiao, H.-Y. & Brimhall, K. C. (2016). The promise of diversity management for climate of inclusion: A state-of-the-art review and meta-Analysis. *Human Service Organizations: Management, Leadership & Governance,* 40(4), 305–333.

Nahapiet, J. & Ghoshal, S. (1998). Social capital, intellectual capital, and the organizational advantage. *Academy of Management Review*, 23(20), 242–266.

Olesen, K. G., Thoft, E., Hasle, P. & Kristensen, T. S. (2008). *Virksomhedens sociale kapital. Hvidbog.* København: Arbejdsmiljørådet og Det Nationale Forskningscenter for Arbejdsmiljø.

Osborne, S. P. (2006). The new public governance. *Public Management Review*, 8(3), 377–387.

Portes, A. (1998). Social capital: Its origins and applications in modern sociology. *Annual Review of Sociology*, 24, 1–24.

Portes, A. (2000). The two meanings of social capital. *Sociological Forum*, 15(1), 1–12.

Portes, A. & Vickstrom, E. (2011). Diversity, social capital, and cohesion. *Annual Review of Sociology*, 37, 461–479.

Prusak, L. & Cohen, D. (2001). How to invest in social capital. *Harvard Business Review*, June, 86–93.

Putnam, R. D. (1995). Tuning in, tuning out: The strange disappearance of social capital in America. *Political Science and Politics*, 28, 664–683.

Rothstein, B. & Stolle, D. (2008). The state and social capital: An institutional theory of generalized trust. *Comparative Politics*, 40(4), 441–459.

Schein, E. H. (2010). *Organizational culture and leadership*, 4th edition. San Francisco, CA: Jossey-Bass.

Skågeby, J. (2010). Gift-giving as a conceptual framework: Framing social behavior in online networks. *Journal of Technology*, 25, 170–177.

Szreter, S. (2002). The state of social capital: Bringing back in power, politics, and history. *Theory and Society*, 31(5), 573–621.

Szreter, S. & Woolcock, M. (2003). Health by association? Social capital, social theory and the political economy of public health. *International Journal of Epidemiology*, 33(4), 650–667.

Thygesen, N. T. & Löfvall, S. (2020). *Gaveøkonomi. Ny vel til bedre velfærd.* [Gift economy. A new way to better welfare]. Leck: Gyldendal Public.

Whitener, E. M., Brodt, S. E., Korsgaard, M. A. & Werner, J. M. (1998). Managers as initiators of trust: An exchange relationship framework for understanding managerial trustworthy behavior. *Academy of Management Review*, 23(3), 513–530.

Woolcock, M. (1998). Social capital and economic development: Towards a theoretical synthesis and policy framework. *Theory and Society*, 27(2), 151–208.

5 Relational Trust and Social Capital in Practice

While the main thrust of this book is to theorize the workings of trust in relation to public sector management and governance, we also want to convey a more elaborate sense of how the theoretical edifice resonates with practical developments on the ground. Our focus in making this connection more tangible will be the Danish public sector, including developments in the realm of trust reform. As previously mentioned, though, Denmark is not the only country where trust has become a label for reforms aiming to debureaucratize and decentralize the public sector. We also see this in neighboring countries Sweden and Norway.

Developments in Sweden mirror the Danish trajectory in the sense that the underlying problematization of New Public Management (NPM) and controls run rampant is very much the same (see Rothstein, 2001, on the Swedish legacy with regard to social capital). However, the Swedish model of implementation is arguably more centralized and government-controlled than the Danish model, reflecting different administrative traditions. The Swedish model has involved the centralized appointment of a "Trust Delegation" (Tillitsdelegationen) that was operative from 2016 to 2020, supporting and facilitating trust-based governance and management at the state level – among government authorities. The Trust Delegation worked closely and experimentally with six authorities in so-called Trust Workshop settings, and it also extended an invitation for all government authorities to join a "Trust Network", which 44 out of 300+ chose to do. The Trust Delegation has involved formalized collaboration between government and the research community, and the starting points and outcomes of its work are documented at length in reports from SOU (Statens Offentliga Utredningar) (2018, 2019). The most recent report concludes that the work on trust has resulted in a number of improvements, ranging from more effective workflows and improved employee motivation to better and more flexible service offerings and improved knowledge sharing with other actors. It concludes that there is now, due to initiatives under the trust umbrella, a stronger and more solid basis for governing with trust, as the leadership of many government authorities has come to recognize its relevance. However, the report also suggests that there is a need for continued and improved dialogue about trust – both vertically and horizontally and through collegial

DOI: 10.4324/9780429431104-5

learning and collaboration. There is a need for long-term commitment and continued government support (perhaps a shared platform) for the trust agenda to succeed (SOU, 2019). In other words, it is a learning process and a continued journey. It is a journey that the Norwegian government has only very recently (in the early months of 2022) committed itself to more wholeheartedly – having looked to Denmark and Sweden for inspiration for a number of years prior to this commitment.

The Danish journey, with regard to reforms and explicit attentiveness toward public sector trust, goes back to around 2008–2009. Developments have arguably been less centralized and have had more of an arm's length and multilevel orientation than what is the case in Sweden. As mentioned in Chapter 1, our aim is not to present the Danish case as a best practice, benchmark or example to follow in other countries. However, we do believe that the Danish trajectory can provide inspiration for development of management and governance practices in other social contexts, and discussion of its manifold manifestations is certainly valuable for a critical and constructive understanding of what makes or breaks trust and trust-based initiatives. Needless to say, government, government agencies and public organizations are constantly exposed to public scrutiny with regard to T1 and T2 relationships, but in keeping with the remainder of this book, our focus in this chapter will almost exclusively be on T3 relationships and thus trust *within* the public sector. Speaking of trust-as-reform in a Danish context, the discussions have mainly centered on T3 relationships.

Importantly, in approaching practices of trust, we do not want to give primacy to its explicit manifestations and how trust has been woven – and continues to be woven – into different reform efforts. While reforms come and go, the risks and opportunities of trust are mainstays of management and governance. Thus, our experience from teaching the messages of this book to professionals over a number of years is that trust provides an opportunity to rethink conventional notions of public management – regardless of whether people have had close encounters with reform efforts under the banner of trust. The relational narrative regarding trust, social capital and gift exchange is one way to challenge ingrained and taken for granted assumptions regarding public administration, management and motivation. As should be apparent from our discussions of power and social capital in Chapters 3 and 4, this narrative is closely intertwined with notions of relationality and relational leadership theory more broadly. More importantly, however, it also resonates with management practices and mindsets. At least that has been our experience over the years, through interactions with hundreds of public managers.

To iterate, the relational approach does not constitute some hallowed ground where normative idealism is allowed to reign supreme and power relations are short-circuited or fade into the background. It does not offer any easy answers or quick fixes. While we believe, as suggested in Chapter 1, that the strength of this approach is that it is well aligned with the practical challenges facing trust in modern organizations, it does make the message of trust less straightforward and more complex and blurry – compared to the perspective of moral trust. Again, this can be part of the explanation for the resonance we have encountered among professionals: The point is that trust is important – not that it is an easy or straightforward proposition.

Speaking of the experience of professionals and of how we approach practices in this chapter, the so-called *research-teaching nexus* is absolutely crucial (Willcoxson et al., 2011). In fact, teaching-based insights have served as a resource throughout the book. Thus, we want to make a virtue out of research-based teaching and how different forms of feedback from professionals can in turn inform scholarly understanding – to the point where we can start to talk about *teaching-based research* and how inputs and knowledge acquired through teaching can serve as guidance and affirmation of academic work (vis-à-vis the double hermeneutic). Two things are worth noting in this regard: (1) when we speak of affirmation, we are referring to two types of insight and feedback. First, that relational trust designates actions and ways of thinking about management and leadership that professionals can identify with and see themselves in – regardless of whether trust is seen to be fashionable and high on the reform agenda at a given moment. Second, that the problematization of extant theories and practices of public administration brought about by the relational trust narrative is considered, valid, relevant and in touch with experiences on the ground; (2) our experience of research-based teaching and how it can intersect with teaching-based research has suggested that experiences of trust (and distrust), power and control differ depending on the type of public organization and professional area of expertise. This is hardly surprising, but it is a problematic that we have not touched upon earlier in the book. Our treatment has thus been based on the assumption that it is meaningful and valuable to apply general theory and general theorizing to the public sector. This is the case, for instance, when we speak of the workings of governance archetypes – the classical or Neo-Weberian bureaucracy, NPM and New Public Governance – and how they are interrelated. The prevalence of such archetypes is symptomatic of how the public sector has increasingly, over the last 20–30 years, been subject to standardized forms of management and governance. This in turn ensures that there are common denominators and points of orientation that make sense across the board, not least frustrations with the workings of NPM. However, the point remains that the trust problematic is conditioned somewhat differently in different parts of the public sector and that, speaking of practices, we need to address such particularistic enactments, that is, different starting points, institutional framework conditions, critical events and resulting trajectories.

Keeping in mind our focus on the research-teaching nexus, we start out with some broad, teaching-based reflections on how trust is enacted in different professional areas of expertise – based partly on our interactions with public professionals over a period of more than 10 years. After this, we provide an outline of the activities that were supported with funding via the formal trust reform agenda (from 2013 to 2016). As we shall see, these activities were mainly focused on experiments with external bridging and thus aiming to support collaboration across organizational boundaries.

Speaking of trust-based leadership and trust reform internally, we then turn to developments within the grand apparatus of the Municipality of Copenhagen, which has housed – and continues to house – a wide variety of trust-based initiatives. In home care, we find one of the most interesting trust initiatives within the Municipality of Copenhagen. We provide a more in-depth analysis of how trust-based reform has made a difference in a low-skilled service area that is often besieged by management control and documentation requirement and to some is the very epitome of NPM in action (Vallentin & Thygesen, 2017a). Finally, we position this case in light of the most recent reform efforts in Denmark centered on trust and debureaucratization.

Sector Enactments of Trust

To iterate, our experience from teaching and interactions with public managers suggests that many experiences of trust are shared across different types of public organizations and professional areas of expertise while others are more particular and related to specific sectoral conditions and developments. In two areas in particular, we can point to critical events that tend to frame people's understanding of (dis)trust. These are the areas of public health and the public school system. In the area of *public health*, in particular with regard to medical treatment in hospitals, we have experienced a widespread interest in social capital and relational coordination (Gittell, Godfrey & Thistlethwaite, 2012) – as a counterweight to bureaucracy and documentation requirements. However, a critical event in the public health system is the advent of *The Health Platform* (Sundhedsplatformen) – a standardized IT system that was implemented from 2016 to 2017 and is meant to support paperless workflows and generate qualitative and quantitative improvements in treatment continuity and patient safety. Although The Health Platform is meant to enable efficiency improvements of clinical processes and workflows to the satisfaction of patients and staff, it is often experienced as overly bureaucratic and inflexible as it saddles doctors, nurses and other medical staff with documentation requirements that can seem meaningless or unnecessary. Another critical event and symptomatic example pointing to dissatisfaction with bureaucratization in public health pertains to the area of psychiatric treatment, where a case of overmedication in a local treatment center in 2012 (the so-called Glostrup case) led to the implementation of new control and documentation requirements for the entire area. These requirements are widely experienced as reflecting distrust toward professionals in psychiatry and their professional judgment.

Overall, the debureaucratization narrative is strong among health professionals, who also tend to have critical opinions about NPM. This reflects a system that is subject to an enormous number of rules, regulations and attendant documentation requirements and performance indicators that are meant to ensure patient rights, transparency and manageability. It is also a very complex and dynamic system that is under continuous pressure to perform and very visible and exposed to public scrutiny when it fails. Speaking of debureaucratization, there is particularly among nurses a strong interest in social capital and relationality – an interest that may or may not be considered as gendered (vis-à-vis our discussions in Chapters 3 and 4). Hospitals are generally known for their professional specialization and for housing strong professional groups and group identities. These include doctors, nurses, porters and administrative personnel. Among these groups, it is often the nurses who take the lead when it comes to supporting collaboration and bonding or bridging social capital – as it is part of their training to consider patient well-being not just in biomedical terms but also as a social and psychological matter. Besides, it is part of their professional expertise to consider the organization of work. The medical profession (doctors) is not, as a rule, relational with its focus on individual bodies and illnesses calling for diagnosis, treatment and cure. This does not preclude, of course, that individual medical doctors in management positions can believe in trust and drive a trust agenda. A recurring theme in efforts to reform the health system and hospital workflows is putting the patient and patient well-being at the very center of things. This requires collaboration and coordination to ensure that patients do not feel lost on their way through the system – where transitions between different functions can be critical, in particular for the most vulnerable patients. Bridging social capital and relational coordination are two ways to address and work toward ameliorating such concerns (see below). Concerns about coordination problems and lack of coherence in the public health system are constantly raised by patients, relatives and patient organizations. In all fairness, though, it is a system that is under enormous and continuous pressure, where resources (economic and human) always seem to be insufficient compared to needs and where economic cutbacks are a constant challenge to social cohesion and provision of quality treatment.

Whereas the implementation of The Health Platform in some (not all) Danish regions and hospitals constitutes a critical event in the health system, the starting point for discussions about trust in the Danish *school system* is quite different. The critical event, as far as the management and governance of primary schools go, is the very public and hotly debated labor market conflict of 2013 that was resolved through a much maligned government intervention following a lockout of teachers. The intervention and subsequent agreement effectively served to make working conditions for school teachers more similar to the agreements for other professions with regard to working hours and compensation. This was widely considered as a win for the employer side (Local Government Denmark and municipalities) and a resounding loss for the employee side (the teacher's union and teachers) – who saw it as a betrayal of the Danish model of labor market negotiation and a public humiliation of the teaching profession. The collective agreement of 2013 is thus a collective trauma that continues to haunt manager–employee relationships in many primary schools. This was followed by a primary school reform in 2014, which, on the one hand, served to standardize teaching in public schools, including the number of weekly teaching hours in different grades, class sizes, teaching plans, uses of pedagogical support and pedagogical goals, required teaching competencies, and use of national tests as a governance tool. On the other, it aimed to strengthen and professionalize school management, thus giving school principals an expanded mandate to lead and make local decisions, not least regarding teachers' working hours. This model is well aligned with notions of self-management and distributed leadership. From the outset, however, a vital ingredient was missing, namely, trust – due to the trauma of 2013 and how it became intertwined with school reforms. The teacher's union was very vocal in questioning the license and abilities of school principals to lead, and found the old model of system trust (in collective agreements) more desirable than local and social trust in managers. Subsequently, school principals have had to work to build trust and establish trusting relationships anew with teachers and union representatives, with differing experiences and varying levels of success.

Speaking in general terms, it arguably goes for education, research and academia more broadly that many professionals in these fields have a preference for the model of "trust" described by Le Grand (see Chapter 3) – that is, a model characterized by professional autonomy and absence of intrusive governance – with freedom from outside interference of any kind as the ideal (and NPM as "the ultimate evil"). However, there does seem to be a generational element to this, with younger professionals being more prone to appreciate that management (and perhaps even governance) can make a positive difference – and that self-management requires management to function properly (vis-à-vis our discussion in Chapter 3). The implementation of teaching teams in primary schools is an example of a model of work that breaks away from the highly individualistic and self-centered model of professional autonomy, calling for relational competences among teachers and for managerial support. Likewise, in academia, we do see tendencies toward valorization of organizational citizenship behavior (investments in social capital, common projects and the common good) – alongside individualized performance indicators. On the one hand, we do not associate the trust agenda with nostalgia and a return to how things used to be in the past, but rather with the making of a present and a future marked by smarter and more effective balancing of trust, power and control. On the other, we do acknowledge the need for trust-based critique of the influx of NPM-inspired governance in education and research, including tendencies toward marketization, disaggregation and decomposition of performance into atomistic, measurable and benchmarkable units – to the detriment of the overall sense of meaning and purpose and the relational requirements of building effective work units and strong working environments.

The area(s) of education and research epitomize the need for distributed leadership and trust (Spillane, 2005), as it is impossible to micromanage this sort of knowledge work. For many of the public managers we have engaged with, trust boils down to a question of how to manage the self-management of highly skilled professionals. In central government agencies, this challenge pertains to the management of highly skilled knowledge workers within bureaucratic systems and entrenched chains of command. Here, part of the managerial challenge is to find ways to change or disrupt conventional modus operandi and look beyond determinants of hierarchy and market for possible benefits of more trust-based solutions. One interesting feedback we got from a middle manager in a central planning function was that he felt that all his colleagues would benefit from engaging in discussions about trust in general and the relational challenge to institutional and economic trust in particular – because it provides a valid and relevant problematization of taken for granted notions of governance, management and motivation in the public sector. Keeping in mind the bias against (social) trust that characterizes parts of the public administration literature (see Chapters 1 and 2), it is worth noting that professionals in central planning functions tend to have a background in economics, political science or law, and that neither of these disciplines are, from the outset, very accommodating as far as benefits of social trust go. Another master student, with an economics background, read the relational narrative as a sort of deconstruction or debunking of, again, neoclassical economic theory and attendant notions of economic governance. To focus on trust is one way to shine a light on unmeasured (perhaps unmeasurable) organizational losses from frustration, friction, demotivation and increased employee turnover that can result from decisions that may seem perfectly sound and valuable from a purely economic perspective – effects that may be invisible to the language of economics and the tools of economic governance. This in turn points to an important function of the relational narrative: as a mode of *problematizion* of existing forms of governance and their managerial and practical implications. Instead of reflecting how things (already) are on the ground, the relational trust narrative can point to development potentials and new ways of thinking and acting in public organizations.

This also goes for developments in *the police* and *armed forces*, both types of organizations that are known for their hierarchical and bureaucratic organization. Our experience is that trust can lead to productive conversations about management and governance even within organizations that are supposed to be overdetermined by hierarchical relations. There are always rooms and spaces where trust can make an important difference and serve to supplement authority, power and control. Moreover, trust is also a way to problematize the workings and implications of NPM and economic and other reforms in the police and armed forces – and in other types of public functions with a strong hierarchical imprint. Functions like *job and employment* and *immigration* services are variations on this theme. These functions are not only highly politicized and minutely regulated, they are also reflective of a relatively high level of distrust toward citizens (T2). This creates a system and culture of rule-following and documentation that arguably leave little room for social trust to make a difference.

After these broad reflections on sector-specific starting points for trust (we address developments in other sectors below), we will now enter the realm of trust reform as it has unfolded in Denmark.

Experimenting with Trust

This section focuses on three projects that were established and received funding via the collective agreement trust reform in 2013. The aim of the three projects, as outlined in a report from KORA (Danish Institute for Local and Regional Government Research) (Hjelmar, Bjørnholt & Christiansen, 2016), was to develop new ideas for governance with a focus on trust and collaboration. The projects took place from 2014 to 2016 and were described as governance labs aiming to showcase how public organizations at the municipal, regional (hospitals) and state level can develop new forms of governance and collaboration based on the principles of the reform (of which trust is one – see Chapter 1). The project thus indicates a need for what is now increasingly referred to as joint or shared public management and strategy (Greve, 2019) or network governance (Klijn & Koppenjan, 2016).

The first project, a so-called *Subacute Offer* (Subakut tilbud), was a collaboration between Nordsjællands Hospital (under The Capital Region of Denmark) and two municipalities in the North Zealand area (Frederikssund and Halsnæs). The project allowed for patients to be diagnosed at the hospital, in the acute care unit, and then get outpatient treatment in their own home, under the auspices of the municipality (the municipal home care). The purpose was to avoid particularly elderly people getting hospitalized with acute illnesses that can be either prevented or treated in their own home. The second project is called *FriNova* and is part of a local psychiatric center under The Health and Care Administration of the Municipality of Copenhagen. The purpose is to help psychologically vulnerable citizens with guidance and support, and through user involvement give them a better sense of coherence and forthcomingness in the public health system. FriNova offers a number of support vehicles and courses coordinated by an internal project manager and carried out by volunteers (most often with user experience) and collaborating NGOs with psychiatric expertise in the local area. Together with user involvement, it is thus the collaboration with other actors that is central to this project. The third project is a collaboration between Kriminalforsorgen (the Danish probation service) and the Municipality of Esbjerg. The project is meant to circumvent that young people (18–30 years of age) waiting to serve time in prison return to criminal activity when they are released. The period between sentencing and serving can in many cases seem long and be experienced as a sort of limbo. If young people do not, in the meantime, get help with their personal finances, work situation, substance abuse treatment, housing situation and so on, there is a risk that they will be in a worse situation when they are released than when they were sentenced. It is a problem that no one has been aware of before, neither in Kriminalforsorgen nor in the Municipality of Esbjerg. Kriminalforsorgen is not informed about what kind of support young offenders are offered when they show up to serve a prison sentence, and the municipality is not automatically informed about verdicts. This makes collaboration imperative. Focus has been on setting up coherent processes, including possibilities regarding education, employment and continued substance abuse treatment during prison time. These efforts are meant to contribute to a good release and to support the individual on his or her journey toward a life without crime (Hjelmar et al., 2016).

Overall, the three projects focus on relationship building between public organizations, user/citizens and other actors in support of welfare state prerogatives – that is, social capital as external bridging. The report from KORA points to a number of important learning points. With regard to the first project, trusting relations between the hospital and municipalities are all-important if the collaboration is to succeed. From the point of view of hospital personnel, this requires knowledge and insight into municipal health offerings so they can feel safe leaving patients still in treatment in the hands of the municipality. It requires ongoing dialogue and communication between the parties to build a sense of security and trust. Such efforts can be successful, but the collaboration is fragile because, particularly in the hospital, there is a lack of familiarity with this way of working (together), and collaborative relations and personal acquaintances between the hospital and municipalities are limited. It is therefore important that the collaboration is supported structurally through management involvement, formal (written) collaborative arrangements, economic incentives and so on. The project has given the municipal home care greater responsibility for the health treatment of citizens. While this is experienced as positive and motivating in home care, it also brings with it new professional requirements and need for upskilling (Hjelmar et al., 2016). We return to these points in our case on home care in the Municipality of Copenhagen.

Building on this, and going back to our discussion of the enactment of trust in the public health system, Danish parliament has, as of June 2022, passed a new health law that mandates the establishment of so-called *health clusters* (Sundhedsministeriet, 2022). The law is meant to support collaboration between hospitals, municipal health care and general practitioners and to be a "motor of implementation" for efforts to create a more coherent health system and take better care of patients. There will be 22 clusters in all, centered on emergency hospitals, and the new law commits the parties to collaborate. The law will come into effect as of July 2022, and it will be interesting to see how this sort of mandated collaborative health reform will play out, accompanied by limited supportive funding (DKK 80M) and new administrative structures and processes involving political and professional levels. Will these developments mark a break away from bureaucratic silo thinking or be caught up in processes of rebureaucratization (see below)?

Getting back to trust reform experiments, experiences with FriNova suggests that horizontal collaboration between the municipality and other actors with psychiatric expertise can support the goal of ensuring that citizens with psychiatric illnesses get better treatment. However, there are a number of challenges involved in making such collaboration work in practice while embracing a more holistic perspective. This collaboration is also fragile, not least because it is dependent upon individuals and personal relationships, without much in the way of management and structural support. It is important that the collaboration is confirmed and maintained on an ongoing basis, not only through personal contacts but also through concrete and communicable positive results that future activities can build on. To establish a common and agreed upon professional basis for the joint endeavor is another big challenge as the field of psychiatric treatment is diverse and characterized by different professional fractions and understandings of mental illness. Besides, there is an experience of organizational barriers between different parts of the health system: municipalities and regions. The analysis from KORA suggests that a rethink of governance and practical solutions in this field requires a dedicated managerial effort and support as there is a need to create free spaces where employees can use their professional expertise and experiment with new ways of delivering public service. As part of the FriNova project, employees have been given leeway to develop, over longer periods of time, their way of working without having to document results or having clearly set goals – an obvious instance of trust-based leadership. Overall, experiences with FriNova have confirmed that a higher degree of user involvement can serve to support citizens' sense of responsibility for their own situation and strengthen the experience of quality in psychiatric treatment. However, the project has also shown that it is difficult to measure the effect of such a social effort with many involved participants, and that it is important to consider how results can be documented and to assess what works and what does not. In other words, there is a need for further development of measurement and documentation (Hjelmar et al., 2016).

The collaboration between Kriminalforsorgen and the Municipality of Esbjerg also illustrates the importance of focusing on results. The collaboration has been driven by employees in both organizations that have shown great commitment with regard to helping a group of vulnerable youths and making a concrete difference (vis-à-vis the notion of public service motivation). Shared goals and focus on the needs of particular groups of citizens can thus serve to break down barriers to collaboration/external bridging. The project has shown that it enables professional engagement and responsibility when decisions can be made in close contact with the youths, and be adapted to their individual needs, while the project at the same time caters to the project participants' experiences and professional expertise. Support from all organizational levels has helped secure positive outcomes. There has been good support from management (reflected in funding for a dedicated administrative position for the project) and from employees, and there has been, across hierarchical levels and between the involved organizations, openness and willingness to contribute to the project. However, the experience has also been that it takes time to establish new forms of collaboration – even if there is a shared focus on creating visible results. The development phase has been relatively long, and it has been used to establish trust between employees and departments in Kriminalforsorgen and the municipality. Finally, parallel to FriNova, it is ultimately found to be difficult to document effects of the effort, as effect studies methodologically require consideration of a number of variables/conditions or factors that are outside the professional frame of the projects (Hjelmar et al., 2016).

In sum, across the three projects, KORA's analysis points to the importance of creating a professional free space or room to maneuver for public employees along with opportunities for collaboration across sectors – based on trust. In all three cases, it has been challenging to establish collaboration across organizational units and established hierarchies, but the projects have shown that such collaboration, with citizens and citizen needs at the center, is a great resource and has great potential when it comes to creating more appropriate and coherent ways of treating ill, elderly, weakened and vulnerable citizens. KORA's analysis also suggests that shared goals can serve to drive collaboration and be supportive of the involved employees' motivation and trust toward each other (Hjelmar et al., 2016). At the time of writing, FriNova and the collaboration between Kriminalforsorgen and the Municipality of Esbjerg are still functioning while the Subacute Offer in North Zealand has been abandoned. However, the subacute model has been adopted by The North Denmark Region, indicating a sort of joint learning process among regions.

Trust in the Municipality of Copenhagen

The public trust agenda has attracted a considerable amount of attention over a number of years and has, in various ways, reflecting different levels of ambition, been formally adopted at state, regional and municipal levels. An explicit starting point for reform efforts under this heading has been a perceived need to free municipalities in particular from the shackles of centralized government control. Thus, it is not surprising that it is municipalities that have tended to take the lead on trust and social capital (although some regions have also been very vocal about their ambitions in this regard). While our focus in this section is developments in the Municipality of Copenhagen, it is important to note that other municipalities around the country – including the cities of Aarhus, Aalborg and Odense – have also articulated ambitious policies and engaged in activities aiming to liberate public employees and make their work life more meaningful and less preoccupied with control and documentation requirements. Some of these policies make explicit use of the term "trust" (often within the frame of "Social Capital" – see Chapter 4) while others cover the same ground without using it.

Before digging deeper into developments in local and national government, we need to clarify what kind of trust reform-based trust is. In essence, trust reform designates *a form of institutional trust-building that is meant to enable social trust in and around public organizations*. Unlike the classical or Neo-Weberian model of governance that turns trust into a background variable, trust reform is an example of how institutional trust can be supportive of post-bureaucratic developments, often in project-based, innovative and conspicuous ways. Trust reform is reflective of institutional change processes, including experiments with new forms of management and governance, and combines top-down and bottom-up perspectives. Thus, there tends to be a certain openness to trust reform (vis-à-vis Foucauldian notions of power as predicated by freedom). Its top-down manifestations are not very concrete or detailed (or binding) as they build on the assumption that solutions are best found locally and through decentralized processes. Trust is not something that can be decided upon or dictated by political leadership or top management, and the supposed strength of an open reform is that it provides ample opportunity for initiatives that are attuned to local conditions and address local problems bottom-up. Trust reform can, on a positive note, serve to legitimize trust-based initiatives in municipalities, regions and administrations – and thus partake in creating more favorable institutional framework conditions for trust to flourish (vis-à-vis the Swedish experience). On a more critical note, however, it is not exempt from the general sense of reform fatigue in the public sector. Besides, being a form of institutional trust aiming to support social trust, trust reform makes use of a dual repertoire of arguments. While the ends are often described in relational terms, the means are about effecting changes to structures, rules and norms – often under the banner of debureaucratization. As we shall see, such efforts are not free from the bureaucratizing pull of hierarchy and thus the problem of rebureaucratization (see Chapter 4). A problem that arguably gets bigger the more centralized initiatives get. We return to this problem at the end of this chapter. For now, we will get back to the local case of Copenhagen.

The Municipality of Copenhagen is with its seven administrations and approximately 45,000 employees Denmark's largest employer. It is also an example of a public body that has made very active use of the trust vocabulary, both in policy statements and organizational initiatives. Thus, Bentzen (2015) identifies no less than 29 examples of trust-based initiatives in the municipality. These include (1) initiatives at the political level, (2) initiatives across administrations, (3) initiatives in particular administrations, (4) initiatives in local organizations and (5) initiatives involving shop stewards and labor agreements. As she points out, the Municipality of Copenhagen may be considered as a "least likely to succeed" case of trust-based management and governance due to its size and organizational complexity. However, as she argues, if trust can succeed here, the likelihood of it succeeding in other settings should be greater. It is a valuable case not because it is representative, but because of the high level of ambition on display (Bentzen, 2018).

At the political level, a *Code of Trust* was adopted by The Copenhagen City Council in 2013. It is meant to provide direction for trust-based initiatives in the seven administrations. According to the code, the trust agenda is meant to assure that employees have more room to deliver quality services and produce public value. The focus on trust, professionalism and smarter solutions is also meant to increase job satisfaction. The removal of ineffective forms of governance is supposed to make it possible for employees to devote more time and resources to core tasks – to the benefit of citizens. For this to work, however, commitment is required both from the political leadership and the seven administrations. Thus, the message to politicians is that they need to have the courage to forego of detailed regulation and make it possible for local aberrations (cases of wrongdoing etc.) to be handled locally instead of through new and generalized control measures. This in turn requires proper investigation of the extent and severity of each single case and, as a rule or default, support for local managers based on trust. Furthermore, the political leadership must continuously strive to weed out superfluous strategies, plans and policies and to question documentation requirements while looking for ways to abandon or simplify them. Bentzen's (2015) analysis suggests that the Code of Trust has made it less legitimate for politicians and political leadership to apply the knee-jerk reaction of command and control when something goes wrong while also more generally problematizing use of power in the form of very detailed regulation.

At the level of administrations, the code suggests that there needs to be a focus on professionalism and effect goals rather than burdensome process goals. However, it is also pointed out that efforts to support and create room for trust in the service encounter to some extent will be constrained by economic and legal framework conditions. It is the task of top management to ensure that such constraints are minimized so that there is room for professional discretion around core tasks. Moreover, it is highlighted that trust is about creating an open dialogue culture allowing for different viewpoints and disagreement. The municipality can thus gain from being able to approach cases starting from multiple perspectives and opinions. An organizational culture that recognizes different viewpoints will ideally allow for a richer, more holistic treatment of cases and provide a stronger basis for making sound decisions while supporting professional development in relation to core tasks.

Across administrations, with The Finance Administration serving as governing or coordinating body, the main focus has been on debureaucratization efforts aiming to, vis-à-vis the Code of Trust, weed out or simplify existing policies, rules and documentation requirements. Other cross-cutting initiatives worth mentioning are an analysis of trust barriers in the municipality and management training in trust-based leadership. On a more action-oriented note, a project aiming to "free" institutions ran from 2014 to 2016. It involved four administrations: The Children and Youth Administration, The Culture and Leisure Administration, The Health and Care Administration, and The Social Services Administration. In each of these administrations, four to six organizations have, during a trial period, been freed from a number of internal rules that they have found burdensome and nonoptimal for the carrying out of their core task. These organizations, which have voluntarily chosen to be part of the experiment (by submitting an application), have served as a sort of laboratory for welfare management as they have been given the opportunity to experiment, for a while, with having fewer rules to adhere to and thus more room to act and exercise professional discretion. The idea being that the experiences gained during the trial period can lead either to permanent release from said rules or to a modification of rules if that is considered more appropriate. Most of the projects have been continued and many solutions have been made permanent throughout the municipality. However, Bentzen's (2015) analysis also points to the existence of communicative barriers. The dialogue between administrative top management and organizations is made difficult by the lack of a common language, and "freeing" has in some organizations led to expectations of total emancipation (trust as an absolute mandate) instead of the proposed liberation from particular bureaucratic rules and requirements.

With regard to initiatives in particular administrations, these have also included debureaucratization efforts. For example, The Health and Care Administration accomplished a reduction of the number of guiding documents from 850 in 2014 to 227 in 2016. Guiding documents include descriptions of workflows, help documents, instructions and guides in relation to care and practical help. The criteria for removing documents include the following: (1) the challenge they are meant to alleviate is associated either with low risk or low prevalence, (2) common sense is expected to work better than a document and (3) the challenge lies within the employee's professional expertise and discretion. Other initiatives include methodological freedom in efforts to reduce sick leave (The Children and Youth Administration) and a new model of governance in home care (The Health and Care Administration) that we provide a more elaborate account of in the next section. Initiatives also include projects focusing on dialogue-based management (The Children and Youth Administration), principles of trust and formalized processes for assessing the meaningfulness of controls and treating cases of unwanted procedures and rules brought up by managers or employees (The Social Services Administration).

In The Culture and Leisure Administration, a former Director experimented with the explicit use of trust as a governance paradigm. He merged organizational units in order to create a flatter organization with fewer hierarchical layers. The reduction from 125 to 25–30 organizational units with each manager referring directly to the board of directors was meant to support decision power close to the action and to citizens. Experiments were, as already mentioned, made allowing organizations to be freed from particular rules found to be burdensome. Procedures aiming to minimize reporting and documentation were also implemented. Thus, managers were only required to report on sick leave, job satisfaction and finances to the board of directors. And they only had to report if the results deviated from prior agreements. Consequently, these issues were usually not reported, but brought up during annual performance appraisal interviews and otherwise, with regard to sick leave and job satisfaction, taken care of by HR. This model was accompanied by a managerial duty to take initiative, report problems and ask for help in critical situations. The Director, wanting to create a culture where managers dared to take chances, also implemented a so-called two error rule for managers. According to this rule, managers were incentivized to commit and report on two errors annually, and not just minor or random mistakes but well-considered, strategic errors indicating a willingness to take risks and dare to act and fail. The Director has described the process of trust reform as learning by doing and laying the tracks while the train was running, without having a master plan. The new decentralized model has created new challenges with regard to governance and organizational coherence – and has in many instances made coordination and knowledge sharing more difficult within the administration. The new model is, for better or worse, very dependent on local managers' willingness and ability to lead in a spirit of trust. However, developments in The Culture and Leisure Administration serves to illustrate how trust can inspire creative rethinking of management and governance practices (Vallentin & Thygesen, 2017b).

Trust remains on the management and governance agenda in the Municipality of Copenhagen. In 2017, The Health and Care Administration adopted a new management codex entitled "Trust at the center", presenting trust as the center of gravity around which managerial values and priorities are organized. However, the most significant current reflection of the trust agenda is the "Charter for working communities" that was adopted by The Finance Administration and subsequently all the other administrations in 2019. The charter explicitly builds on and supports the municipal trust agenda and its imperatives regarding employee involvement, codetermination and coresponsibility as vital for the provision of quality services and overall job satisfaction. Another way to understand the charter is to see it as a translation of the trust agenda into a related placeholder agenda (working communities and *management of* working communities) that may be easier for employees to identify with and which may be more helpful in directly addressing the needs of citizens. This is one way to try and overcome some of the general barriers to trust-based management and governance that Bentzen (2015, 2018) points to in her analysis. These include structural – horizontal and vertical – barriers, problems of mobilizing resources during busy workdays, lack of competencies and motivation, communicative barriers (due to the manifold meanings of and expectations evoked by trust) and old habits: new structures do not automatically lead to a new work culture, and this has to be taken into account in the assessment of trust-based initiatives. Trust-based reform is a process that takes place over time. It is not a quick or simple fix – as our case concerning trust-based developments in home care also illustrates.

Trust-Based Reform of Home Care

Home care is part of The Health and Care Administration, which is the municipality's largest in terms of annual budget (DKK 6.4 billion) and employees (approximately 10,000). Home care provides health care or protective care to people in need, in particular senior citizens (aged 65+). It has approximately 1,200 employees and consists of five operational units covering local boroughs, and 40 operational groups. It makes 8,700 visits to users every day, which amounts to 10% of all home care that is carried out in Denmark. This section uses and expands on the case as presented in Vallentin and Thygesen (2017a). The case as presented here only captures part of the complexity involved in the management and governance of service delivery that is covered by two separate sets of legislation (regarding *Health* and *Service*) and attendant institutional requirements and administrative practices.

The trust agenda was first set in motion by the former Mayor of Health and Care, Ninna Thomsen from the Socialist People's Party, who used reform of home care as an election promise when running for office in 2009. She communicated an urgent need to get rid of detailed regulation and the control mentality that has become dominant after many years of governance dictated by NPM. The trust and social capital agenda has subsequently been brought to bear in a number of different initiatives within The Health and Care Administration. Central among these is the implementation of a new governance model for home care.

To begin with, the new model does not constitute a radical departure from the prior model. It is rather a hybrid model containing elements of institutional, economic and relational trust. Provision of home care was – and is – organized through an NPM technology that creates an internal quasi-market by separating the *ordering* and the *delivery* of services in order to benefit *receivers* (the so-called BUM model). Home care services are ordered by a visitation function whose task it is to assess the needs of users. Visitation thus serves as the public authority that decides which services users are entitled to, and operations (or other, private service providers) then makes deliveries. The new governance model does not change this basic principle. Instead, it reduces the number of specific units (work tasks) designated in the management of home care while introducing *visiting blocks* as a more open and trusting means of governing without compromising control.

Prior to the reform, the management of home care specified no less than 79 individual units/deliveries (the exact number is contested) and home care professionals had to register their use of time on a handheld computer, a so-called PDA: personal digital assistant. Registration included their check-in time for work, their coming and going in each user's home and their lunch break. In internal communications, the new governance model has been presented as a radical administrative simplification, and the transition has been framed as putting an effective end to the "time and control tyranny" in home care. The time tyranny has ended in the sense that home care professionals no longer have to register how they spend their time. They have been relieved of this administrative burden and this should better enable them to be mentally present, caring and attuned to the individual needs of users – apart from actually having more time for the core task of delivering care.

Visiting blocks embrace the whole service encounter and this means that home care professionals have been given more freedom to manoeuver and exercise their professional expertise and judgment. Visiting blocks basically refer to the time of day when service is delivered: morning, middle of the day and evening. However, depending on the needs of users, the content stipulated in visiting blocks can be "light", "moderate" or "comprehensive". Moreover, a distinction is also made between "early" and "late" evening, making it possible to specify special needs for support in visiting blocks (particularly for elderly people suffering from dementia or other cognitive ailments). When all is accounted for, the new model defines 19 visiting blocks (the most recent update, as of 2020, includes a couple of additional content categories, but the concept essentially remains the same). Included in visiting blocks are services such as helping the user get dressed and move around, personal hygiene, toilet visits, baths, light cleaning and waste disposal, serving of breakfast and other meals, along with help in eating and drinking. On top of this, a number of services are given specifically to users (i.e., they are not included in visiting blocks). There are 21 of these in all and they include help with medicine (taking of medicine and opening of medicine bags), transportation outside the home, shopping and social visits and telephone calls. In addition, many of the deliveries included in visiting blocks can also be given as specific services if users have additional needs that cannot be accommodated within the time span of visiting blocks. What has been accomplished, in sum, is akin to a 50% reduction in managed units: from 79 (services) to 19 (visiting blocks) + 21 (services) = 40.

With this new model, work plans as a means of control are not discarded, but home care professionals are given considerable leeway with regard to how they spend their time in users' homes: they can choose to prioritize one task over another, or they can choose to spend more time with one user at the cost of others on any given day. In all, however, they have not been given more time to do their job, which arguably puts pressure on their ability to manage their own time, avoid giving favorable treatment to particular users, and so on. Instead of time registration, home care professionals now have to make a daily and weekly work plan and coordinate this with users based on their needs. This reflects how visiting blocks are also meant to accommodate better user dialogue and inclusion of citizens. The work plan is an administrative burden on employees, but serves an important professional purpose as it should make it easier for temporal workers to do a good job, that is, one that is attuned to the needs and expectations of the individual user. This is important in order to assure consistency, which alongside user satisfaction is a crucial performance indicator for trust-based initiatives (as their effects can be difficult to measure directly).

However, the easiest part of visiting blocks is implementing it as a new structure. The hard part has to do with the process of change in organizational culture that must follow. This is not only a matter of home care professionals adjusting themselves to a new, more self-managing mindset. It is also a matter of redefining what the management of home care is about. In other words, it involves creation of new managerial and employee identities.

Visiting blocks is supposed to allow managers to have more of a professional focus without losing control. This is an important part of trust reform in home care as it entails an increased reliance on professional judgment calls and new uncertainties and responsibilities associated herewith. As part of this effort, managers are supposed to engage more closely with employees and how they do their job. This includes occasional observation of how home care is being carried out in users' homes. Ideally, employees should perceive this supervision as part of a professional dialogue, but it can also be perceived as undue interference, signaling distrust and an unwelcome need to look over the shoulder of employees. There is a challenge here for managers to (re)assert themselves in terms of their professional expertise – after many years in a system preoccupied with administrative paper work, documentation and control. Part of the learning process has to do with creating a new, more professional dialogue between managers and employees that is based on trust and a mutual understanding of the new governance model and its possibilities. The process of implementing the new governance model is bound to proceed differently in different parts of the organization. As mentioned, home care consists of five local units and 40 operational work groups with 40 group leaders. The local units cover different boroughs, and the different work groups and their leaders and employees to some extent reflect the different cultures and user profiles found in different parts of Copenhagen. No central efforts are made to streamline – or control – how different managers cope with the challenges related to trust in regard to their employees and there is an acceptance that there can be strength in diversity.

Different managers have different prerequisites for succeeding with this endeavor. The new model signals a higher degree of trust in relation to home care professionals and it opens a space for managers to manage in a manner that is more conducive to the creation of trusting relationships. However, it is up to the individual managers to figure out how best to fill this space and balance trust and control. There is a high level of awareness in the organization that managers are not automatically imbued with trust just because trust initiatives and trust reform are on the organizational agenda. They will each have to deserve the trust of employees. Hence, some managers have not been able to live up to the new professional requirements. In the words of a home care manager:

> There are managers who have not been able to live up to [the new requirements], and it has very much been related to the trust agenda. Those skillful managers that we found very useful 10–15 years ago, who were very militaristic: "this is what you must do, now just go out and do it", some of those we have had to get rid of. There is no doubt that there is a need for managers with professional capacity, who can, perhaps through delegation, lift the professional task. (Vallentin & Thygesen, 2017a, p. 160)

This is indicative of how the new model has served to create new managerial roles and identities. It comes with a new set of professional requirements and demands for managerial action. This creates new challenges for managers to navigate in the nexus of trust and control. The same goes for employees in operations. Among employees, the new model has generally been a success story as it represents a welcome softening of the stronghold of NPM that comes with promises of better performance, better care and happier and more motivated employees. Many home care professionals experience more freedom in their daily work life. This makes it easier for them to be mentally present and attuned to the needs of users. However, the implementation of visiting blocks is not necessarily associated with trust as such – that seems to depend on how strong relations are to the immediate supervisor/manager. Skepticism has been detected among some employees, whose reaction is related to negative experiences of prior reform efforts. This is another indicator that trust-based forms of management may not be experienced as such – and may not be successful in creating trust. Whether or how it does is ultimately an empirical question. In parallel, users are most often not aware of the coming of visiting blocks, not to mention their embeddedness in the trust agenda. What is important is that they are satisfied and experience consistency in the delivery of services.

With freedom comes responsibility. The event of visiting blocks and the reconfigured relation between operations and visitation mean that home care professionals are exposed to new professional demands. Apart from delivering care, the job of home care professionals is now also to continually observe, register and communicate the changing needs of users. The new model has thus added complexity and created a more demanding job, and this is very much experienced in the organization. The new model implies a further professionalization of home care (other reforms have also been pulling in this direction), making employees with longer education in social care and health more valuable compared to low-skilled workers. Home care is often associated with routine and manual tasks, but the new model adds an element of knowledge work to the list of tasks and skills required. The knowledge work requires not only certain professional qualifications, but also the ability to communicate professional judgments and argue your case. Many low-skilled employees are finding these requirements very challenging, and management is making an urgent call for these employees to further educate themselves, train and upgrade their skills. Experimentation with self-managing teams in home care points in the same direction: it calls for upskilling and managerial support. Better educated employees are better equipped to make professional judgment calls: they can act as nurses, when there is a need for it, and in some cases, they have also been given the task of observing homes that are covered by low-skilled colleagues. However, home care is now facing dire recruitment problems, and therefore, the push for more skilled employees has turned out to be untenable.

While the new model can nevertheless exclude some, it can also support new forms of inclusion and responsibility. Home care is subject to budget cuts, and it is therefore imperative to stay within the budget in the different parts of the organization. In one working group, the employees made a common vow to avoid (costly) use of temporary help and to cover for each other when a colleague called in sick. They succeeded in bringing the use of temps down to zero, and this can be seen as an example of how strong social relations and holistic thinking (albeit at a local level) can have positive performance and economic effects. Although this initiative is not directly a result of the trust reform, it reflects the kind of responsible professionalism that the new model is meant to promote. Control is not sidelined, but formal control is supplemented by local social control.

On a more conflictual note, the reform first showed signs of increasing tensions between visitation and operations by tipping the scales and altering the power balance between the two. Arguably, the trust reform makes it more legitimate for operations not only to call for more time to do a proper job with users, but also to challenge the NPM-dictated authority of visitation in home care altogether. The extant organization of home care installs a principal-agent relationship between visitation and operations. In the resulting division of labor, it is not the function of visitation to have trust in home care employees, but to supervise and control the quality and delivery of services according to extant rules and regulations. A former head of visitations argued that her approach, as public authority, was political and economic – focusing on what citizens require and what political object-ives are at stake. She also found that she was meeting and negotiating with people from home care with very different approaches to care. She found that group leaders would sometimes use trust as a sort of "club" (weapon) to legitimize the need for more time to do their job, thus using trust as an argu-ment in discussions that, according to her, had nothing to do with trust, but was all about economic and professional requirements. This clash between system trust and social trust imperatives is reflective of how visitation is not supposed to have a holistic outlook on the organization of home care. It is supposed to close focus on each discrete service offering and the contractual means by which it can best be delivered. However, this conflictual view does not adequately reflect how relations between visitation and operations have developed after the implementation of visiting blocks.

Both in visitation and operations, managers and employees have had to adapt themselves to the new model. In operations, employees have gone through a learning process of finding out how best to work with visiting blocks, while in visitation they have gone through a process of adapting to the new, less-controlled conditions for delivery of services. As expressed by one home care manager, "time has been helpful". Even if the extant model creates oppositional interests between the parties, time has seen fewer conflicts and more flexibility and tolerance emerge in relations between visitation and operations; thus, there has been a sharp reduction in the correction of services that individual users are entitled to. This was supported by a change of management in visitation. The new manager came with a greater belief that trust can be an economic benefit for the organization, and that home care employees have the abilities needed to lift their new respon-sibilities. This has resulted in greater mutual understanding, recognition and respect for each other's ways of doing things. This has in turn provided a basis for much better collaboration between visitation and operations. These effects show how categorical differences that come with particular models of governing can be softened and to some extent reconciled in hybrid practices, and thus point to the need for a process-based, relational understanding of the trust-control nexus.

In sum, the new governance model by no means constitutes implementation of trust in a uniform manner. Instead, as we have seen, it creates multiple open spaces for trust and control to emerge and be negotiated between organizational members in novel ways. With regard to managers and management processes, an illustrative example is the event of supervision in home care. We cannot attribute an unequivocal trust or control value to supervision beforehand. The relationship between trust and control emerges out of individual encounters between managers and employees and is bound to be perceived differently by the involved parties. For employees, the use of visiting blocks comes with new freedoms as well as new responsibilities. It creates a more demanding job that is also meant to be more fulfilling for employees. How these altered working conditions translate into trust and control is an empirical question that calls for more in-depth empirical study.

Current and Future Perspectives of Trust Reform

The trust reform is ongoing – a work in progress, so to speak. Over the years, the same basic effort has been given many names. Apart from "trust", Danish governments have been engaged in efforts to effect a "coherence" reform, a "debureaucratization" reform and a "proximity" reform, arguing for the need to apply an arm's length principle and let more decisions be taken locally. The current Prime Minister, Mette Frederiksen from the Social Democratic Party, has, in consecutive opening speeches to parliament (2019–2020), spoken of the need for legislators to dare "let go" (2019) and for members of parliament to get their "hands off" the public sector, even when mistakes are made (2020).

A preferred governmental way to drive this agenda has been to experiment with the freeing of municipalities from extant rules and regulations (so-called Frikommuneforsøg). The first round of such high-level experimentation ran from 2012 to 2015 and included nine municipalities. The second round ran from 2016 to 2020 and included eight networks of (up to six) municipalities; its focus was thus on collaboration and bridging activities. Both rounds have been based on a principle of voluntariness – through submitted applications from municipalities and networks expressing a desire to participate. The third and latest round was set in motion in 2019 and involves new welfare agreements related to day care, primary schools and elder care. The conditions of freedom, if you will, are written into new "Laws on welfare agreements" that were passed in 2021. Their expressed aim is to free the governance and management of day care, primary schools and elder care in selected municipalities in order to "create more room to act for employees and managers in support of quality, professionalism, care and presence" – to the benefit of citizens.

As indicated, these experiments only pertain to selected municipalities – seven in all, specified with regard to the three public service areas: day care (the municipalities of Helsingør and Rebild), primary schools (Esbjerg and Holbæk) and elder care (Langeland, Middelfart and Viborg). The seven municipalities are currently engaged in 200 local trials, experimenting with new ways of organizing welfare (Hjelmar, Pedersen & Tranæs, 2022). The fact that this opportunity is written into law indicates that it is one of the more bureaucratic modes of trust reform and can involve considerable administrative burdens (as some evaluations have shown). However, the supposed freeing of municipalities does send a strong political signal about the importance of debureaucratization and has led some mayors to talk of the possibility of "starting over with a blank slate" – freed from layers of entrenched and ineffective red tape. With freedom comes responsibility, though, and while the municipalities in question have considerable methodological freedom when it comes to determining which rules to hold onto and which to discard, they are expected to deliver results that are as good as or superior to the results they delivered before engaging in such experimentation. And they will no longer, to the same extent, be able to blame the central government if something goes wrong and its performance does not live up to expectations.

As a final important point of this chapter, the Danish government has vowed to extend this freeing exercise to all of the 98 Danish municipalities as per 2022, which can potentially lead to a considerable multiplication of experiments taking place. In her televised New Year's Speech on January 1, 2022, Prime Minister Mette Frederiksen addressed the basic problem of rampant bureaucratization:

> The picture is the same in large parts of the public sector. Too much time is spent on process, bureaucracy, control and formulars. It tears away at job satisfaction. It makes it hard to recruit. And it results in welfare that does not always live up to expectations. It is time to find a way into the core. What is most important for our welfare? Relations, presence, care and professionalism. A welfare society where there is more room for the heart than for control. More common sense than regulation.
>
> (author's own translation from Statsministeriet, 2022)

The Prime Minister has addresses the trust issue on multiple occasions, but this time, she showed an apparent willingness to push developments further than before. Thus, she went on to make a new commitment regarding trust, freedom and self-determination in elder care:

> hand on the heart, we do not yet have the elder care in Denmark that our elderly deserve. Tonight, I will therefore make a far-reaching proposal. That we get rid of the voluminous regulation and legislation in elder care and start all over. A new and precise Elderly Act. With clear values. Dignity. Freedom of choice. Self-determination. And minimal documentation requirements. Let the employees use their good heads and warm hearts. Let us, as relatives, spend more time together with our elderly. Let the elders get the love and care that they need in the Autumn of their life.
>
> (ibid.)

While the Prime Minister only mentions elder care in her speech, the new proposal is taken to mean freedom to "start over" for all municipalities in regard to not only elder care, but also day care and primary schools. The experiment of freeing municipalities will no longer be a contained exercise, applying to only a few local areas; it will be rolled out countrywide and thus supposedly involve greater risks and opportunities. It is still too early to make even qualified guesses with regard to outcomes. However, the proposal does beg a number of questions. Keeping in mind that the freeing of municipalities is not an end in itself, but a means to better serve public needs, what kind of impact will this initiative have, not only on the development of public organizations and their practices, but also on the assessment and comparability of their performance and ultimately their accountability – toward central government and local citizens? How many municipalities and projects will be allowed in, and how deep cuts will they be allowed to make – for better or worse? With new freedoms come new responsibilities: How many municipalities will have the will and courage to take this step, and how enabling or constraining will they find the process to be? How blank a slate will they be able to accomplish, and how will debureaucratization efforts stand in relation to rebureaucratization outcomes? What kind of effect can multiple projects, experimentation and resulting outcomes in these particular areas have for the general development and standing of trust in the public sector? What we can say with certainty, based on our theoretical treatment and the cases of this chapter, is that there is still a lot of work to be done and a lot of difficult challenges ahead. Underneath the purity of political rhetoric and popular calls to replace control with trust, there is a more complex reality involving ongoing interactions, negotiations and tugs-of-war between trust, power and control.

References

Bentzen, T. Ø. (2015). *Tillidsbaseret styring og ledelse i offentlige organisationer – i springet fra ambition til praksis.* [Trust-based governance and management in public organizations – In the leap from ambition to practice]. Ph.d.-afhandling. Roskilde: Roskilde Universitet.

Bentzen, T. Ø. (2018). *Tillidsbaseret styring og ledelse i offentlige organisationer.* [Trust-based governance and management in public organizations]. Højberg: Jurist- og Økonomforbundets Forlag.

Gittell, J. H., Godfrey, M. & Thistlethwaite, J. (2012). Editorial. Interprofessional collaborative practice and relational coordination: Improving healthcare through relationships. *Journal of Interprofessional Care*, Early Online: 1–4. DOI: 10.3109/13561820.2012.730564.

Greve, C. (2019). *Fællesoffentlig ledelse. Hvordan offentlige ledere skaber sammenhæng i den offentlige sektor.* [Shared public leadership. How public managers create coherence in the public sector]. København: DJØF Forlag.

Hjelmar, U., Bjørnholt, B. & Christiansen, A. M. (2016). *Nye styre- og arbejdsformer som led i moderniseringen af den offentlige sektor.* [New forms of governance and work in the modernization of the public sector]. København: KORA.

Hjelmar, U., Pedersen, C. S. & Tranæs, T. (2022). Statsministerens historiske frihedsforsøg åbner et fuglebur – men hvordan får vi de bedste resultater? [The prime minister's historical experiment with freedom opens a birdcage – but how do we get the best results?] *Vive.dk*, Debatindlæg, January 26.

Klijn, E. H. & Koppenjan, J. (2016). *Governance networks in the public sector.* Oxon: Routledge.

Rothstein, B. (2001). Social capital in the social democratic welfare state. *Politics & Society*, 29(2), 207–241.

Spillane, J. P. (2005). Distributed leadership. *The Educational Forum*, 69(2), 143–150.

Statens Offentliga Utredningar. (2018). *Styra och leda med tillit – Forskning och praktik.* [Governing and managing with trust – Research and practice]. Stockholm: SOU 2018:38.

Statens Offentliga Utredningar. (2019). *Med tillit följer bättre resultat – tillitsbaserad styrning och ledning i staten.* [With trust comes better results – Trust-based governance and management in the state]. Stockholm: SOU 2019:43.

Statsministeriet. (2022). *Mette Frederiksens nytårstale 1. januar 2022.* [Mette Frederiksen's new year's speech] Downloaded from www.stm.dk/statsministe ren/taler/mette-frederiksens-nytaarstale-1-januar-2022/

Sundhedsministeriet (2022). Sundhedsklyngerne skrives nu ind i sundhedsloven. [The health clusters are now written into the health law] *Sundhedsministeriet pressemeddelelse, June 9.* Downloaded from: https://sum.dk/nyheder/2022/juni/ sundhedsklyngerne-skrives-nu-ind-i-sundhedsloven

Vallentin, S. & Thygesen, N. (2017a). Trust and control in public sector reform: Complementary and beyond. *Journal of Trust Research*, 7(2), 150–169.

Vallentin, S. & Thygesen, N. (2017b). *Tillid, magt og offentlige ledelsesreformer.* [Trust, power and public management reform]. Riga: Akademisk Forlag.

Willcoxson, L., Manning, M. L., Johnston, N. & Gething, K. (2011). Enhancing the research-teaching Nexus: Building teaching-based research from research-based teaching. *International Journal of Teaching and Learning in Higher Education*, 23(1), 1–10.

6 Trust, Leadership and Technology
Old Conundrums and New Openings

This final chapter will be used to briefly take stock of and reflect on the fundamentals of trust and trust-based leadership while also opening up a couple of additional and supplementary themes and some current and future general reflections. First, we address the fundamental question of *what trust is* and what can be said about this based on the insights of the book. Second, we address the question of *what trust-based leadership is* in more general terms. With a couple of closing nods to Luhmann, we then engage in some final reflections regarding embodied (*repersonalized*) and disembodied (*depersonalized*) trust. With regard to the former, and continuing on the leadership path, we use the notion of *managerial self-presentation* to show how trust plays into personal leadership and to summarize the overall challenge to modern management posed by this book. With regard to the latter, we provide a brief discussion of how trust is related to technological development in general and new digital solutions in particular. Important points being that there is, as a rule, always an analog (human, behavioral, social, relational) dimension to digitalization, and that even supposedly "trust-free" technologies are to some extent conditioned upon trusting relations. Finally, we conclude with some reflections on hopes and fears and possible future developments for managerial trust.

What Is Trust?

Altogether, this book has strived to clarify the different – direct and indirect – ways in which trust is addressed and becomes a managerial and organizational concern in the public sector. It is important to understand that trust is not an unequivocal management or governance rationale, but can take on different meanings depending on the paradigmatic assumptions one subscribes to. In this book, we have argued for the value of an understanding of trust that is both relational and inclusive – that is, an understanding that embodies certain normative ideals while also being able to observe and recognize other – institutional, economic, moral – vantage points and thus how other understandings, based on different sets of assumptions, partake in creating the layered social and organizational realities of trust. Speaking of social reality, we have strongly emphasized the social conditioning of trust – as

DOI: 10.4324/9780429431104-6

opposed to trust as a psychological state or cognitive orientation. This is not to deny the importance of people's individual experiences and mindsets regarding trust. However, from a sociological and relational point of view, individual experiences and psychological states always need to be considered in context and as socially conditioned. That being said, we certainly advocate an ecumenical and complementary approach to the study of trust, which, as previously mentioned, sits at the boundary of sociology and psychology. Importantly, the choice between a psychological or a sociological starting point is not just a matter of ontological and/or epistemological assumptions and allegiances in some dry and formalistic scientific sense. It is a matter of connectivity and what types of reflections a particular choice of perspective opens up to. A social and relational vantage point allow us to consider the sociopolitical implications of trust, and thus how assumptions regarding trust are embedded in theories, archetypes and tools of management and governance. Instead of seeking to explain patterns or effects at the individual level (in individual psyches), we have explored how trust is at stake in the social realm (involving both impersonal and personal carriers of trust), how it intersects with power relations and control and how it is subject to tugs-of-war involving vested interests and conflicting theoretical and professional allegiances. While the book has certainly provided advocacy for the normative and instrumental merits of (relational) trust, it has also shown how trust is a political matter, ripe with tensions and ambivalences and involved in struggles over the hearts and minds of public sector managers and employees.

What Is Trust-Based Leadership?

In this book, as in others, you search in vain for a short and succinct definition of what "trust-based leadership" is. Trust-based leadership (or management) is not a well-defined or clearly delineated conceptual construct or form of practice that is easily distinguishable from other managerial concepts or practices. We can highlight certain management principles as closely intertwined with trust, and we can point to certain authentic and transformational leaders as people who seem to embody ideals of trust – but trust-based leadership is difficult to contain as a particular thing or a pure form. This can be part of the reason why organizations tend to avoid using and committing themselves to this particular terminology. You are arguably promising less when committing to a "trust agenda" than if you claim to practice "trust-based leadership". The workings of organizational trust are, as we have argued throughout the book, closely intertwined with governance and control and thus the money (market) and the power (hierarchy). Some will tend to see these close affiliations as symptomatic of how trust imperatives in practice tend to be overpowered by other, more material organizational concerns, indicating that there is no great hope or potential to be found in trust.

This book has proposed a more accommodating and balanced yet optimistic approach, the starting point being that trust is always, in one way or another, relevant to management and to managers and makes a difference even when it is absent. Indeed, our inclusive approach has shown how theories of trust apply even to managers who would never think of it. There is a need to challenge extant forms of management and governance in the public sector through the use of concepts, models and mindsets that provide more room for trust and more room for self-management and collaboration involving managers and employees. In what relations and spaces can trust make a positive difference? How can more trust-based tools of management and governance supplement or replace others? Developments in this realm cannot be contained within a concept of trust-based leadership. This book has suggested that it calls for a broader and relational – theoretical and practical – engagement with governance paradigms and associated practices, post-bureaucratic organization and post-heroic leadership, social capital and gift exchange.

Another problem with the notion of trust-based leadership is that it connotes heroic leadership qualities and may thus lend support to a myopic view of the modern leader as the ultimate source or cause of organizational trust. That is the case if or when trust-based leadership is seen to be something that only formal leaders engage in – a unidirectional (top-down) practice connecting strong leaders with ardent followers. Notions of shared, distributed and post–heroic leadership suggest that there are alternatives to such myopia. However, our discussion of these notions brought up the issue of gender and how post–heroic leadership is often associated with traits that are considered as feminine or socially attributed to women. While the literature on trust and management and organization is blind to the issue of gender, the literature on post–heroic leadership can to some extent serve to fill the gap. It suggests that post–heroic leadership is sometimes associated with powerlessness and therefore tends to be less apparent and less visible in organizations. This would seem to require a rethink of what kind of leadership figures are seen to embody trust – from the transformational alpha male or female, to more subtle and facilitating operators (female, male or beyond).

Even though we have strongly emphasized the shared or distributed properties of management, it is, even from a relational and sociological point of view, relevant to reflect on the risks and opportunities that trust entails for individual (formal) managers and personal leadership. With a nod to Luhmann, we will address this as a matter of *managerial self-presentation* – thus taking the argument back to the individual and personal trust, albeit the individual and personal trust *in context*.

Managerial Self-Presentation

Luhmann's take on personal trust provides a thought-provoking perspective on the social properties of managerial trust and the hall of mirrors regarding expectations and attributions that modern management takes place in (cf. Sørhaug, 1996). According to Luhmann (2017), personal trust is the generalized expectation that the other will handle his freedom, his uncanny potential for diverse action, in keeping with his personality – or, rather, in keeping with the personality which he has presented and made socially visible. He who stands by what he has allowed to be known about himself, whether consciously or unconsciously, is trustworthy.

(p. 43)

The defining characteristics of this definition are 1) contingency (the explicit dependence on the freedom of the other), 2) the focus on experience-based expectations regarding the other (as opposed to the emotions of the trustor or the personal qualities, as such, of the trustee), 3) the emphasis on the social persona as the addressee of trust and as a product of conscious as well as unconscious social appearance and 4) the focus on trust as a matter of predictability (although, as we have argued, this part needs to be restricted to positive expectations regarding ability, benevolence and integrity).

As Luhmann points out, the motives behind the actions of an individual may be of widely different kinds. A person may be concerned to appear worthy of other people's trust or he may make an effort to appear true to himself, thus making self-respect the highest priority. He may act spontaneously and allow his personality to function as an unconscious selection mechanism. In any case, in spite of the variety of possible motivations, a similar result is forthcoming, a selective presentation of self, which provides other people with criteria on which to build trust (or the opposite). This selective self-presentation, however, is a social product, not just a reflection of the conscious and purposive strategies of the individual. Every conceivable kind of behavior says something about the person behaving, and an individual, through his behavior, actions and decisions, "always gives away more information about himself than he can reconcile with his ideal self and more than he consciously wants to communicate" (Luhmann, 2017, p. 44).

How do these properties of personal trust apply to the sphere of managerial action, then? Managers present themselves in every social doing they are involved in, but the meaning of these doings is determined by others. Managerial self-presentation, in this sense, is not the same as the articulated self-understanding of managers. It is true for managers as for others that they do not have ownership over their personal appearance. The social persona is a social product that comes into being and develops through interaction with others. It cannot be shaped at will and does not always correspond with the ideal image of who the manager wants to be or would like to think he or she is in the eyes of others. Therefore, the articulated self-understanding and the stories that managers tell about themselves only provide a two-dimensional understanding of the problem of self-presentation. Managers may seek to control or manipulate the perceptions of others, but in the final call, self-presentation cannot be purposely controlled. It works behind people's backs, so to speak, incorporating conscious and unconscious ways of acting along with formal and informal stories – about flattering and less flattering actions, decisions and sequences of events, the front stage and the backstage, what can stand the light of day and what perhaps cannot. Managers are in principle "on" all the time, even when they prefer not to be. There is no place to hide as even inaction can be considered a form of action and affect the level of trust.

Generally speaking, managers strive to draw a consistent picture of themselves and to make this picture socially accepted. However, "self-presentation is difficult, threatened by inner contradictions, mistakes, facts, and information which cannot be presented. So, on the one hand it requires considerable expressive prudence and, on the other hand, the tactful co-operation of the spectators" (Luhmann, 2017, p. 90). Delicate or embarrassing situations may arise if it appears that the presented self (as articulated by the manager) is not the real or true self, if the manager says one thing and does another (ibid.).

Different strategies can be applied in situations where promises are obviously broken or principles obviously breached. The situation may be given a humorous twist, open admission may be an option, or the incident may be downplayed and more or less ignored as an event of no particular importance, for instance, as a disturbance caused by external, unforeseeable events. Moreover, it is possible for managers to build up goodwill over time, which can give them some credit on the trust account and ensure or at least increase the likelihood that even negative experiences can be interpreted positively or forgiven. Managers and employees do not start over with each other all the time. On the basis of experience, the parties build up expectations toward each other over time, and this process may be based on a necessary acceptance that the future is unknown, that things do not always go as planned and that people (managers included) make mistakes. In light of the all too obviously bounded nature of human rationality and judgment, trust and loss of trust will in many instances be relative rather than absolute measures. Self-presentation is not something static. In dynamic social contexts, the self-presentations of participants are continuously evolving. It may take a long time to build up trust, and it may, in particular grievous instances, evaporate instantaneously following a single act perceived as a betrayal. Trust must be created and maintained continuously. The credibility and trustworthiness of self-presentations are at stake all the time, and it involves *factual* (professional or managerial qualifications) as well as *social* (social competencies and emotional intelligence) and *temporal* (reliability and consistency over time) aspects of managerial performance.

Luhmann argues that trust can accumulate like a form of capital (vis-à-vis social capital) and can serve as a form of social control undercutting tactical prospects of deception. He writes:

> One can win trust by means of deceitful self-presentation, but one can only maintain it and use it as continually available capital if one continues the deception. Illusion then turns unnoticed into reality, the qualities which were at first deceitful grow into habits, the advantages of trust serve as an instrument of obligation. Trust educates. This is true on

the emotional level as much as on the tactical level, and neutralizes the dangers which lie in a purely tactical control of trust relationships.

(2017, p. 71)

Luhmann suggests that "Trust educates", but something is still missing in this argument (as it relates to modern management) and it has to do with the underlying notion of predictability. To argue that managers can be caught up in their virtuous self-presentations, and that this can lead to more or continued trusting behavior and learning, is to assume that the personal qualities of managers that were considered trustworthy and fit for the task yesterday will be considered trustworthy and fit for the task today and tomorrow. More of the same will suffice. With predictability comes the notion or unquestioned assumption that managerial trust can somehow continue to build on traditional and well-established rules and norms relating to authority and heroism, command and control, market and hierarchy – and that the license of established ways of doing things can be extended into the future without further ado. From the point of view of relational trust, such an assumption must be considered as too static or even conservative or reactionary. Not surprisingly, perhaps, considering his theoretical reach, Luhmann is also able to capture the dynamic and constantly changing aspects of personal and managerial trust. Not only does he argue that the creation and maintenance of trust is ultimately an ongoing effort in the present that is never secured by events in the past or future expectations (see Chapter 2), he also provides a formalization of the argument in the language of social systems theory:

> It may be in extreme cases there are people, or social systems, who earn trust simply by remaining fixedly and immovably what they are (…) [This] presupposes an environment which is immovable and neither dangerous nor very complex (…) In a changeable environment (…) this attitude implies dangers for the existence of the system and hence for the continuance of trust, too. Systems which are able to experience the trust they have in their environment as a problem, and are able to deal with it, are more elastic, more complex, and more durable. Their self-presentation becomes more conscious, and adjustable to more complex conditions.
>
> (Luhmann, 2017, p. 66)

To create and maintain trust, it does not suffice to remain the same, do the same and present yourself in the same way. The relational trust narrative thus provides a fundamental challenge to heroic and authoritarian notions of management and their continued relevance and legitimacy. In complex, dynamic and (sometimes) dangerous social environments, managers need to take heed of changing demands and expectations and make adjustments – without losing themselves or compromising their integrity. Part of the challenge can be to embrace "the relational" and the shared, distributed and post-heroic aspects of management along with agendas regarding inclusion, diversity, responsibility and sustainability. Resorting to the answers and rationales of yesteryear, predictable as they may be, will almost certainly not suffice. This is one way to summarize the book's overall challenge to modern management.

Trust and Digital Technologies

From repersonalization of trust to the depersonalization of trust found in the realm of technology: We address technology not just to juxtapose it with personal leadership, but because digitalization plays an increasing role in relations between the public sector and citizens and is ubiquitous in discussions about user involvement and user value. Moreover, "Digital welfare" is meant to enable debureaucratization and better collaboration between public bodies and is in that sense overlapping with the trust agenda. Perhaps digital technology provides more effective answers to some of the problems we have addressed from an analog (social, managerial) perspective. Cutting-edge developments in blockchain technology even promise to provide "trust free" solutions, and thus to decrease our dependence on centralized authorities and institutions as well as social trust. Before getting to that topic, however, we will first turn to the more mundane matter of how digitalization strategies are unfolding in the public sector.

Modern social orders are, as Luhmann (2017) points out, much too complex for trust to rely only on personal relations and individual experience. We have already accounted for this when speaking about system trust. At the societal level, system trust is reflected in trust toward money (as a medium of exchange), science (and scientific knowledge), technology, government institutions and other authorities. For example, to trust in the stability of the value of money (and in continued opportunities to spend money) is normally to assume that a system is functioning and to place trust in that function and not in any individual you happen to know or any personal experience or knowledge. Compared to personal trust, system trust makes learning easier and control more difficult (Luhmann, 2017). This is certainly the case with regard to technology and new digital solutions. The following treatment of digitalization strategies is based mainly on two reports from the Danish Agency for Digitisation (Regeringen & Regioner, 2013, 2016).

Public sector developments are increasingly affected by the many facets of digitalization, including developments of Web 2.0, Industry 4.0, Internet of Things, sharing or platform economy (as a form of gift economy), uses of social media and apps, open-source software and knowledge development, viral networks, blockchain technology, big data and artificial intelligence. The digital economy is a motor for radical innovation and disruption of existing business models and notions of value creation. Apart from its enormous commercial value, it holds great potential for public innovation. In Denmark, this potential has for a number of years been addressed through reports and strategies focusing on the development potential that digitalization has for public welfare. Indeed, "Digital welfare" has been promoted for the last 20 years through various joint public strategies, aiming to support better collaboration and knowledge sharing across administrations, sectors and professional boundaries. The basic idea being that digitalization can provide tools for creating a more effective and coherent public sector, while supporting better inclusion and participation of citizens as users of public services. Among the areas that have spearheaded such efforts are provision of telemedicine, self-service solutions and other welfare technologies in health care, along with more effective case treatment through digital solutions. There is a lot of attentiveness to new user interfaces and possibilities for more direct user contact through use of mobile services, smartphones and tablets. This includes ongoing improvement and development of public self-service solutions and webpages and portals giving citizens easier access to service and information.

This technology-driven support of collaboration and knowledge sharing makes data and data sharing in public welfare a critical concern. How can state, regional and municipal bodies improve their ability to share and reuse data (when considered possible, safe and relevant)? How can public authorities be better at sharing relevant information with each other and to a greater extent automatize case treatment so that the time people need to spend on digital applications and reporting of information is reduced? Better sharing of data should make it possible for citizens to avoid giving the same information more than once and serve to create more coherent processes across state, regional and municipal jurisdictions. Use of digital technology is thus meant to enable debureaucratization through easier and faster processes, and this should in turn help free up time and resources for the provision of core welfare. However, the digitalization of welfare does face a number of challenges related to governance and management.

As pointed out in the most recent joint strategy on digital welfare, the Danish public sector builds on the principle that public service should be delivered locally or regionally within the boundaries of the law, and that this helps support an overall sense of proximity, security and trust in society. It is therefore important that digitalization happens in ways that support local decisions and responsibility along with local inclusion of citizens. In other words, it is important that digital strategies are supportive of local democracy. At the same time, however, it is important for public authorities to ensure that the digital solutions applied are useful across sectors and actors. As much as possible, standards should be applied together with reuse of technology and infrastructure and relevant joint solutions. For example, better reuse of data can be supported through shared data standards and formats and a robust IT architecture. However, this is where the public sector runs into a number of challenges. In many places, it will be necessary to modernize or change IT systems because they are outdated or lacking in functionality. Many public IT solutions and processes are thus built on internal organizational needs and modes of organizing rather than the needs of citizens, and many data are defined and stored in different ways by different public bodies, making it difficult to share data and to collaborate. A considerable work of development and "cleaning up" is ongoing. It is a process that calls for both decentralized implementation capacity and joint public collaboration and coordination of digitalization efforts.

Digitalization has the potential to support debureaucratization and better collaboration, coordination and knowledge sharing between public organizations – across sectors and professional boundaries. With its focus on data and the sharing and reuse of data digitalization comes with promises of much improved user interfaces and user involvement. Does this mean that many of the problems and challenges that this book has addressed from an analog – social, managerial – perspective can be addressed better and more effectively by digital means? With regard to user involvement, there is no doubt that digitalization has unique potential and is superior to other solutions. User involvement on a grand scale can only happen in an effective and flexible manner through the use of digital solutions. Apart from that, however, we need to insert a number of organizational and managerial variables in the technology equation. As indicated by the joint public digitalization strategies, the development of cross-cutting solutions will, apart from the technical challenges involved, be highly dependent on good collaboration and coordination between public organizations and between the state, regions and municipalities. Trust, strong social relations and an open and giving mentality with regard to collaboration and knowledge sharing will be important resources in efforts to make digitalization happen effectively and without undue friction and resistance. Part of the task is to increase the digital readiness level among public organizations and thus the willingness and ability to make digital development happen. This necessarily involves analog questions regarding organization, management and human behavior and motivation.

The same point applies to the development and use of so-called trust-free technologies. Blockchain technology is, through the creation of "an immutable, consensually agreed, and publicly available record of past transactions" supposed to enable "verified and transparent recording and value exchange mechanisms without the need for a central authority or institution" (Hawlitschek, Notheisen & Teubner, 2018, pp. 50–51). However, as Hawlitschek et al. (2018) argue, it is not probable that blockchain will eliminate the need for trust between transaction partners. They show how the notion of a trust-free system tends to be framed within an understanding of blockchains as engineered ecosystems defined solely by their technical properties. However, a more critical and socio-material understanding is bound to reject such a closed and self-contained view of technology (which in this case needs to involve trust in algorithms and algorithmic authority – a dubious proposition as of late). From a behavioral point of view, it becomes clear that human interactions, with all their complexities and "leftover uncertainties", are difficult to integrate in a blockchain without a trusted interface, and that "blockchain technology in and by itself is *not* able to provide an environment that renders trust-building outside the closed blockchain ecosystem obsolete" (ibid., p. 59). In other words, blockchain partakes in changing the landscape of trust and offers innovative and decentralized solutions, but it does not render other forms of trust – or trust altogether – obsolete. They continue to provide a backdrop and impetus for blockchain transactions. The system trust offered by technology is important, but it cannot stand on its own. This brings us to the closing remarks of the book.

Hopes, Fears and Possible Futures

Trust is, no matter how you twist it or turn it, not the solution to all problems and woes in the public sector. Trust is not always the solution, it is not always well-chosen and there are many things it is not capable of. There is a need to draw on many types of solutions and resources. The function of trust with regard to future development is to shine a light on the importance of social relations and a systemic, holistic and collaborative understanding of public organization, public value creation and development.

Our treatment of trust has solid roots in the experience of modern liberal democracy in general and the modern welfare state in particular. With our focus on internal (T3) trust relations, big (T1 and T2) trust issues like anti-corruption, transparency and accountability have been largely absent, reflecting a discourse aiming to strengthen collaboration, increase job satisfaction and better serve citizens. The trust narrative has been less about deterrence (avoiding negative outcomes) than about enabling positive outcomes in the form of managerial and organizational change. Hopeful optimism has loomed larger than skeptical pessimism, although we have tried to steer a balanced and critical course. The question remains, however, how transferable the resulting ideas are to other contexts, where different institutional, social and economic conditions prevail? As we see it, it is not so much a matter of whether, but rather of *how* the book's ideas can be made relevant and put to use in other settings – either as diagnostic tools or as input to driving change and looking for new solutions. After all, its theoretical findings do build on international research that, taken together, transcend any singular local experience.

You can always claim universal relevance by making trust an individual and thus a personal issue. However, in keeping with our relational approach, we do believe that the proposed relational and inclusive framework has general relevance and applicability – not necessarily as a harbinger of reform, but as a means to gain a better and more nuanced understanding of the different meanings of trust – institutional, economic, moral, relational – that prevail in public organizations and how trust is intertwined with power and control. The framework is adaptable to other conditions and can be made to reflect – and respect – different starting points without undue moralizing. Obviously, in many contexts, there is a need to build system trust and support classical bureaucratic values rather than social trust. There are no easy solutions to problems of low or absent trust in administrative systems marred by corruption and self-serving and opportunistic behavior, and, as we have argued, distrust tends to be a self-reaffirming and vicious cycle.

Even under such conditions, however, the proposed framework may be able to shed light on the kinds of trust that persist in different nooks and crannies of the system and what kind of difference it makes. Future empirical studies could include surveys of how the understanding of trust among public managers and employees is distributed between the four paradigms and whether or how differences are related to differences regarding gender, age, culture, professional background and so forth – thus bridging the sociological and psychological research streams. Questions also remain with regard to how the framework intersects with T1 and T2 relationships.

Hopes and fears with regard to trust and distrust are bound to differ from context to context, from country to country and regionally, locally and down to particular organizations. There is certainly a lot work to be done to further the cause, with the trust crisis, as it pertains to governments, politicians and other authorities, being symptomatic of the challenges ahead. Taking the helicopter perspective, we live in a world of rampant polarization and tribalism, marred by post-factual tendencies and whataboutism in politics and public and social media discourse. With this comes a divided politics that threatens meaningful democratic debate and weakens the social fabric. On top of that, we are, alongside economic theories in action in public, private and social realms, seeing how precarious labor and the gig economy are becoming more and more prevalent phenomena. Furthermore, we are witnessing the commercialization and widespread use of control and surveillance technologies by states and private businesses, ranging from China's Social Credit System to the minute monitoring of workers in Amazon warehouses. Indeed, apart from offering supposedly "trust free" solutions, technological development is part and parcel of an additional kind of trust crisis, namely, the one that is reflected in diffusion of modes of management and governance that make a virtue – and business model – out of denigrating trust (or instrumentalizing the economic brand of system trust). It is a self-perpetuating process enabled by technology's ability to partition, measure and produce endless amounts of numbers. The end results are anything but relational, and this is the core strength and fundamental weakness of this type of solution that capitalizes on distrust. Its economic and technical concreteness and supposed effectiveness mask its often inhumane outcomes.

Where does this leave us with regard to trust? It may seem terribly naïve to rely on trust or speak of its merits in a world of distrust. However, it is important to remember that theories, concepts and frameworks do more than reflect social reality. They partake in creating social reality, and part of the problem with the diffusion of distrustful mindsets and technologies is that they are often based on problematic and simplified assumptions about human behavior and motivation (not to mention authoritarian or economic ideology). This is not just the way the world is or the way that people or things happen to be. Like climate change, these are manmade developments, and the question we have to ask is: *What kinds of organizations, what kinds of societies and what kinds of politics do we get if or when trust is allowed to deteriorate or trampled underfoot?* It goes for theory as well as practice and for public administration as well as other realms of organization: surrendering to distrust is not an option. There are alternatives and other possible futures.

References

Hawlitschek, F., Notheisen, B. & Teubner, T. (2018). The limits of trust-free systems: A literature review on blockchain technology and trust in the sharing economy. *Electronic Commerce Research and Applications*, 29, 50–63.

Luhmann, N. (2017). *Trust and power*. St. Ives: Polity Press.

Regeringen, K. L. & Danske Regioner. (2013). *Digital velfærd – En lettere hverdag. Fællesoffentlig strategi for digital velfærd 2013–2020*. [Digital welfare – Making everyday life easier. Shared public strategy for digital welfare 2013–2020]. København: Digitaliseringsstyrelsen. Downloaded from: https://fm.dk/media/14150/Digitalvelfaerd_enletterehverdag_web.pdf

Regeringen, K. L. & Danske Regioner. (2016). *Et stærkere og mere trygt digitalt samfund. Den fællesoffentlige digitaliseringsstrategi 2016–2020*. [A stronger and safer digital society. Shared public digitalization strategy 2016–2020]. København: Digitaliseringsstyrelsen. Downloaded from: https://digst.dk/media/12811/strategi-2016–2020-enkelt-tilgaengelig.pdf

Sørhaug, T. (1996). *Om ledelse. Makt og tillit i moderne organisering*. [On management. Power and trust in modern organizing]. Oslo, Norway: Universitetsforlaget.

Index

Printed in the United States
by Baker & Taylor Publisher Services